The
HAPPINESS
TOOLBOX

Finding Happiness
Regardless of Circumstances

LORI BRANT B.A., B.Ed.
Life Coach

Wholesale discounts for book orders are available through IngramSpark or Spring Arbor Distributors.

If it is your desire to be happy regardless of outside circumstances, go to **http://www.loribrant.com** to learn more about one on one coaching.

ISBN

978-1-77302-025-9 (paperback)

978-1-77302-027-3 (ebook)

978-1-77302-026-6 (Hard cover)

Published in Canada.

First Edition

Table of Contents

ᴄ☾◯☽ᴐ

DEDICATION

This book is dedicated to my family. In memory of my mother and father who I love with all my heart and have missed dearly throughout my life. Thank you for teaching us all how to laugh freely and often.

I would like to thank my sister for inspiring me to be a better person, supporting me through thick and thin, and loving me unconditionally. I am blessed to have you in my life and will be forever grateful for your laughter and everything you have done for me.

Thank you to my brothers for showing my children the loving nature of our father through your presence, essence and laughter.

I also want to thank God for the birth of my children and allowing me to be a part of their lives.

Thank you to my children for enduring my journey back to who I really am. I love you both very much.

ACKNOWLEDGEMENTS

I would like to thank the people who have supported me along the way, Katherine, Patty, Jennifer, Betty and Dwyne, Brenda, Melanie, Karen and Joanne. I treasure my friends and family, the time we had together and the meaning you have all brought to my life.

Thank you to Debbie, Tania, Betsy, Kelly, Janet, Steve and Alison for their feedback on the book.

A special thank you to Dr. Lucette Nadle, who graciously reviewed my manuscript and wrote the beautiful foreword. Her support and kindness inspired and encouraged me.

I am grateful for everyone who has touched my life, if only for a second, because they have each brought me to this very moment.

∾◉◡

FOREWORD

According to the legendary Chinese philosopher Lao Tzu, "the journey of a thousand miles begins with a single step". Lori Brant provides us with the tools to create our personal roadmap to figure out how to take that first step and continue our life journey when we find ourselves derailed and disoriented by traumatic events or just the everyday mysteries and challenges of life on this planet.

Illness, injury, loss of loved ones, relationships/jobs/home or other unexpected life events can leave you feeling lost, as if the proverbial rug has been pulled out from under your feet. This book is a guide to finding your true self, returning "home" to love, life and wholeness when your sense of reality has been completely disrupted, when your sense of self: who you are and how you live in the world is shattered, leaving you with more questions than answers about how to define who you are, how to get into the flow of life, to recognize and allow love/holy spirit/divine light/the health to express itself through you, obliterating that sense of being fractured, lost, and incomplete.

With gentle compassion and humor, Lori powerfully shares her life story, including the diagnosis of a life-changing illness at a young age, living with a "disability". She shares her evolution to wholeness, connected to the love and light that shines in and around all of us. Lori teaches us to open up where we have shut down, to redefine who we are, shedding limiting beliefs that keep us mired in grief and loneliness. She gently leads us to connect with the joyful potency and beauty that is our birthright and is infinitely available to us when we get out of our own way.

This gem of a book is an effective "how-to" manual for taking that first step, and continuing along "The Way," shifting from disability to infinite possibility, for those seeking to crawl out of the emotional and spiritual abyss, as well as for those who seek to understand and support those actively on the journey to wholeness.

For those with the courage and/or desperation to undertake this journey, and for those desiring to understand and support loved ones doing the work toward wholeness, this book provides guidance and support. It's a bumpy road. Lori provides exercises for learning to let go of trying to control what is out of our control and trusting, even without understanding what it is we are trusting in, that we are being caught by eternal love when we fall. She encourages us to open up to working with that unknowable, life-giving potency that connects all of us.

May you be filled with and surrounded by peace and loving kindness, now and forever.

Dr. Lucette Nadle
Doctor of Osteopathy

꧁꧂

INTRODUCTION

This book follows my journey from childhood to the present, through death and disease, from unconsciousness to presence and the strategies I used to get there. I discovered that finding happiness regardless of circumstances was possible but required me to understand three things. One, how my past influenced my present. Secondly, how to identify specific barriers and how to move through them and finally, how to experience happiness and enjoy life's journey without relying on external stimuli.

There came a time when in the midst of a chronic illness, marriage problems and depression, I reached out for resources to help me move forward, and found them lacking. They seemed vague and difficult to apply and didn't create any real change in my life or to the way I felt. I craved a book that could show me what I needed to learn to maintain a state of happiness regardless of circumstances.

I had a Bachelor of Arts degree in Psychology, Bachelor of Education and read hundreds of books. I took seminars, trained to be a Life Coach and a Master Spirit Life Coach, got my Masters in Metaphysics, wrote courses and gave workshops. I was doing what all the books told me to do, to think positively, meditate, eat right, repeat affirmations, but inevitably something beyond my control would happen and send me spiraling backward into chaos and depression. It felt as if I was making changes on top of quicksand. There was something missing.

I discovered that limiting beliefs blocked new possibilities from entering my experience and were sabotaging my efforts to thrive emotionally, mentally, physically and spiritually. When I went looking to eradicate those beliefs, however, I couldn't find them. Since they seemed to be so prevalent and dominant, I expected them to be easy to identify, but I was wrong. Some of the most significant patterns that ruled my life were initially picked up almost through osmosis, undetected, and were emotional time bombs.

It is my hope that by sharing my childhood stories with you, you will see how limiting beliefs manifested in my life and how they may have manifested in yours as well. These beliefs are important because they help to form the foundation of your perception. You might be tempted to jump ahead and skip my story to get to the techniques and strategies straight away, but I would encourage you not to do so. Whatever attempts you make to move forward, set goals, be happy, think positively, make changes or move through illness, those efforts may be thwarted by hidden, limiting beliefs operating subtly, in the underpinnings of your life. It is my hope that you will find a part of yourself in my story, or it will trigger an incident in your memory of an event or events that may be still influencing you today.

It is my desire that by openly sharing my challenges and the strategies I used to deal with a chronic illness it will help you to rediscover who you really are and offer you the desire and tools to move forward, find happiness and live a rockin' life.

If you are like me, I wanted someone to tell me how to heal. Just tell me how to do it and I'll do it.

"You need to change your thinking," they would say.

"What thinking do I need to change?" I'd ask.

"The negative thoughts that made you sick. You must have a belief pattern you believe to be true that is manifesting as illness in your body."

"How do I find out what negative thoughts are making me sick? How do I find these patterns?"

"Meditate."

Well, I meditated, meditated some more and meditated even more after that. I had incredible experiences, sensations and uncovered some patterns, but what I really wanted was to heal.

"Nothing is happening; I am uncovering patterns, but I am still sick. Now, what?"

"The Law of Attraction says you need to identify what you don't want, think about what you do want and love what you have."

"How is it possible to love what you have if you don't want it?"

Everyone seemed to have the knowledge of how a person could heal, but no one could show me how to do it. What they seemed certain of, however, was how **they** could heal me.

They would say, "I can heal you. I have such and such ability, and I can heal you. Have you tried these vitamins, herbs, therapy, exercise, standing on your head or traveling to India to work with a guru?"

The question is, if we all have the ability to heal ourselves, why is it that everyone else seemed to have the capacity to heal me and I didn't? They had an answer for that too.

"If you are not healing, you must be doubting that it is possible. Or, deep down you want to be sick."

"Really? That is why I am not healing? You are saying I want this?"

I began to realize that the only person that could help me heal was someone who saw me as completely healthy, whole and complete just as I was, and that included myself. To do that, I needed to be in alignment with who I really was, and my relationships and illness were leading me to discover the thoughts and beliefs that were keeping me from that. Instead of eliminating unhappiness I needed to focus on BEING happy. As I integrated the tools, implemented strategies and learned to love myself and everything in my experience, I began to reconnect further to the essence of my being. I recognized that the actual desire within me to heal was rooted in the judgment that illness was wrong, less than, bad, something to get rid of and was perpetuated by the belief that I needed to heal to be happy.

I believe my life has been an exploration of my **foundation of perception** which is made up of the thoughts and beliefs in my unconscious that I have accumulated since birth. Gregg Braden (2008), in *The Spontaneous Healing of Belief,* suggested that we absorb information unfiltered until the age of seven. From my experience, I continued to absorb emotionally charged, limiting beliefs after the age of seven as well, without realizing it and those beliefs added to and created cracks in my foundation of perception.

If you are like me, the challenge you are dealing with can seem emotionally and physically exhausting, leaving you in the clutches of the unconscious. This can create the perfect storm where an emotionally charged present day experience collides with an emotionally charged past. You act and think unconsciously because physiologically it is easier for your brain to respond automatically. However, those unconscious belief patterns may be wrought with fear and stress, creating havoc in your life. The challenge you are experiencing today triggers other similar emotionally charged experiences, creating reactions now, that are overcharged and exaggerated. That is why other limiting, learned beliefs and patterns may become more prevalent or create stress in other areas of your life during a crisis.

Illness or relationships do not need to heal for you to be happy but are the mechanisms being used by the universe to bring attention to cracks in your foundation and show you who you really are. Every experience is the perfect experience conspiring to return you home. It is not your body or your partner that needs to change but the limiting belief that they need to. Instead of reacting to what is happening, the Universe is urging you to observe and be present with what is going on. Through presence comes connection and through connection, possibilities materialize.

Loving yourself and everything in your experience entirely, dissolves the judgment of circumstances as good or bad. Once you love everything in your experience, the need for anything to change no longer exists. That is enlightenment. That is who we really are, loving awareness and presence of everything that is.

My journey to true happiness exclusive of anything outside of myself has required me to patch the cracks in my foundation one thought at a time. Step-by-step I felt the fear, challenged my thoughts and surrendered to reality which in turn, strengthened my perceptual foundation and revealed who I really was. I, like you, am pure love. Without a shaky foundation to alter your experience, you have the ability to see everything just as it is; As pure love, including your disease or challenge.

Happiness is possible regardless of outside circumstances because when you love everything, the need of a physical, emotional, mental or spiritual healing is no longer required. Pure love sees only pure love in its reflection.

CHAPTER ONE:
HAPPINESS ELUDED ME

A letter arrived from Laurier in the mail, and I quickly tore open the envelope.

"We are pleased to offer you admission to Wilfrid Laurier University for the 1985-86 school year."

"Whooooo Hooooo, I did it!" My arms jolted up, and my feet danced a little jig as I cheered for my accomplishment. Then I stopped. I looked around my kitchen and out the window at the grated steel walkway and realized; there was no one to tell. I knew I could call my sister or my brothers, but it was not the same. I wanted to tell Mom and Dad. I wanted to see their smiles, their excitement, and their pride, the same way I wanted them there at my birthday party watching me open gifts. I wanted to hear them tell their friends over Rye and Cokes how excited they were about me going to Laurier, how proud they were and that I did an amazing job.

I wanted things to be different, and it hurt.

DIAGNOSIS

I was nineteen and in the middle of my first set of exams in University. The pain in the center of my back was unbearable, so I made an appointment to see the doctor on campus.

"Anything else bothering you?"

"Well, I can't put my arms above my head." I was not sure why I brought that up. It was not something new because I had told Mom about it years ago and she didn't seem too concerned. One appointment led to another, and I found myself in his office, across from him, when I heard him say, "you have FSH-MD (facioscapulohumeral Muscular Dystrophy)."

I saw his lips moving, I knew he was talking, but my body couldn't hear him. It was as though I was in a long tunnel moving through this inner space, further and further away. I stumbled as I got up and backed out of the room, devastated.

I struggled to get home, my head swarming with images of a dilapidated body slouched in a wheelchair, unable to move and communicate. I thought my life was over.

I postponed my exams and stayed with my brother for a month over the Christmas holidays to process the diagnosis. It was explained to me that my muscles would weaken in my face, shoulders and arms gradually over time for the rest of my life.

I was spent. I envisioned myself slumped over the arm of a wheelchair soulless and useless. With Mom's death still fresh, I didn't have the capacity to cope and refused to stay there, even though I could not fathom how I would get through it. I ended up doing what I had always done. Ignored it and pushed it down inside where all the stuff that was too painful to deal with gathered. Refusing to let it change my plans, I went back to school camouflaging the pain, diagnosis, and prognosis with denial.

MARRIAGE AND CHILDREN

In 1989, I graduated from Teacher's College and began my first teaching job.

I wanted nothing more than to fall in love, get married and have a home. Since my parents died, I had moved to and from University, from this apartment to that apartment and from my sister's house to my brother's house, longing for a permanent place to hang my hat and call my own. What attracted me most to my future partner was that he appeared to be settled because he inherited a home from his father. What I also loved was, I felt like he got me. He had lost his father at a young age and nursed him to his death by himself. He told me stories of him dying and how no one came to help. The tragic stories of his childhood echoed the pain and suffering I had felt growing up and that strangely comforted me.

My partner had a way of making me laugh, and we would banter back and forth with sarcasm trying to get the best comeback. I felt worshiped by him in those early days, and he did everything right to gain my affection. He took care of me, making me feel secure, relaxed and loved. We were inseparable and talked for hours around the campfire that first summer. As a husband, I thought he potentially could appreciate and understand all of me, not just the cheerful façade that everyone else knew.

I hoped that one day I would wake up and say I was truly happy, and during that time in my life, I thought I was truly happy. I believed I had what I needed to feel whole.

Both he and I worked full time, and we were busy during the week. On weekends we usually chose to hang out with friends, eat, drink and play cards or board games together. I enjoyed my time with friends but felt a yearning for more. I had a husband, house, a good job and was grateful for that but there seemed to be something missing.

In April of 1992, I had just returned from lunch and was involved in a lesson with my grade 7 class when suddenly I felt tingling and numbness on the left side of my tongue. Instantly, I knew that something must be terribly wrong. I called the office and asked that someone come out to supervise my class, and I drove myself to the doctor's office. By the time I arrived my whole left side was numb, and the doctor indicated that we should call my partner immediately because I could be bleeding in the brain.

By the time the ambulance took me to the hospital the symptoms had subsided and the doctors were perplexed. A stroke seemed odd for a woman who was 26 years old. They transported me to Toronto to see some specialists who discovered from my angiogram that I had a dissection of the left vertebral artery and also confirmed that the TIA (transient ischemic attack) was not hereditary. The hospital documented my muscular dystrophy, treated me with blood thinners, and sent me on my way. No one knew, myself included that this medical scare had opened up my old wounds and the grief buried deep from years earlier had begun to ooze from my pores. They told me I would be fine, but fine never came. I longed for someone to scoop me up and take care of me, to fill the void of my empty shell.

I felt completely drained and incapable of coping with yet another crisis, but routinely and systematically, I picked up the pieces again and within a month my life was back to normal. At least, on the outside, it looked normal, but on the inside, I was a little hollower.

When my partner suggested we try to have a baby, it excited me but sometimes I felt I was too young. Without a mother around I knew I'd be on my own, and I wasn't quite sure I would know what to do. Tragically, but not surprisingly, we miscarried.

"Why me? Why does everything always happen to me?"

We tried to get pregnant again but this time, we were very cautious and didn't tell anyone until we passed the first three months. In January of 1994, I gave birth to a wonderful baby girl. She was healthy and happy, and I believed that my life had finally made a turn for the better and that the days of loss, sadness and illness were behind me. With this new found contentment and joy, we decided to have another child and became pregnant after only six months of delivering my first. My son was born June of 1995, and he too was healthy and happy. What more could a mother want?

I was very fatigued after my son was born. Our children were one and a half years apart so things on the home front were extremely busy. I began noticing that my weak arms were becoming a problem. Carrying children and all their gear was beginning to be a challenge. As the winter approached, I tried my best to adapt to my challenges sometimes putting my son in a sled to get from the car to the house to avoid having to carry him on the slippery snow and ice. It was frightening. I often wondered if I was going to drop him. So many times I had come close. Just before I headed back to work the following January, I had the first of many future mishaps. I fell down a short set of stairs breaking a toe, making the transition back to work even more difficult.

DISABILITY

My job was everything to me. The summer holidays in 1996 were rapidly disappearing and although I usually felt revived and sun-kissed after a few months by the lake, that summer drained me and exhaustion shadowed my every move. The new school year approached, and begrudgingly I prepared for my new position as a special education resource teacher. I no longer had a class of my own, so for the first couple of days I consulted faculty and scheduled their students. It was a fragment of the responsibility demanded of a regular, elementary school teacher.

Each day my physical fatigue intensified. The muscles in my legs, arms, back, and shoulders ached as they hung from their joints and every move exhausted me. Mentally I was depleted. I returned home at the end of the day, longing for a safe place to fall. Finding my partner in the kitchen, I stood in front of him, dropped my head with my chin to my chest and sobbed uncontrollably. He stared at me, silent, stunned and powerless with our children at his side. I wanted him to scoop me up in his arms and tell me he would make everything OK. I wanted him to tell me how much he loved me and how we would work through this together, that he would stand by me no matter what. I wanted him to take care of me.

"I'll take the kids for a walk so you can have some time to yourself, " he said. I felt abandoned, alone, and terrified.

Worn out like a discarded rag doll, I decided to take some time off work until I figured out what was happening. That first Monday after the new school year started was my last.

Reality stared me down as I sat alone on the couch and depression swallowed me whole. Consumed with fear, I begged, "God, please send me an angel." No one came. I felt like a scared little child wanting mommy or daddy to wrap their arms around me and tell things would work out. I wanted help but had no one to call.

Suddenly, numbness crept along the left side of my tongue, face and the full length of my left arm. *"Why me?" How could this be happening...Again? I'm only 30 years old. I was so tired of being in crisis. How much could one person take?* My hand shook as I reached for the phone and dialed 911.

The ambulance arrived and took me to the local Hospital where they performed some quick tests and determined I had had another TIA, the second in the last four years. I was transported to Toronto, where neurologists performed a multitude of tests and concluded that it was indeed a TIA and the pain and fatigue I was experiencing was the result of my muscular dystrophy progressing. Even though they told me it wouldn't happen, the MD had moved into my legs. I was sent home digesting the news that the MD was progressive and that eventually I might require the use of a wheelchair.

I wanted to meet the new challenge head on, get over it, push it down and get on with my life just like I had done so many times in the past. This time, it was different. The pain intensified, and exhaustion followed me. It could not be ignored, and the neurologist willingly signed all the required documentation. Officially disabled, I no longer felt like a contributing member of society. I was no longer a teacher, ...I was nothing.

For four years I stayed home. Sometimes I was able to watch my children, but more often than not they were babysat outside our home because I did not have the stamina, strength or attention needed to take care of them by myself. The nights were endless because I could never get comfortable, my arms regularly fell asleep, my skin ached, my bones hurt, and my muscles throbbed.

I couldn't concentrate on what people were saying because most of my attention was preoccupied with the pain and it wore me out requiring me to nap most afternoons. I tried to reserve my energy by having personal support workers 5 hours each week to help me with cleaning, laundry and grocery shopping but the exhaustion and discomfort were relentless. I avoided stairs at all costs and didn't venture out unless I had to. My whole day seemed consumed with the pain, and I could not fathom how I would fill all the days of the rest of my life. One day just turned into the next and one painful experience drifted into another. Taking Tylenol threes were necessary just to get through the day as the muscular dystrophy caused my muscles to atrophy slowly over time.

Frustrated, upset and desperately trying to express myself, I smashed my fist down hard on the clothes washer lid and yelled. "I fucking hate this!"

My partner, standing just outside the laundry room responded, "if you ever do that again, I am leaving you."

My yearly visit to my neurologist that year was devastating. I was thoroughly depressed, and she recommended that I start taking anti-depressants because there was nothing she could do for me, there were no medications or treatments and my MD (muscular dystrophy) was going to progress continually. My marriage was crumbling, my body was failing, and my life was withering away.

I had two children, a mortgage, partner, and a dog. No one knew how to help me, but they tried. Doctors gave me pain killers, psychiatrists gave me anti-depressants, occupational therapists gave me tools, friends listened, and my family offered support and a soft place to fall.

It did not matter that I had people to love me, people to love back and enough money to take care of myself and my family because it all disappeared into the black hole inside of me without a trace, leaving an insatiable, endless void that ached for something different. I could not verbalize what I needed or wanted because I did not know what it was. It couldn't be named or defined, ordered or formed but it existed. It had to exist. I could not believe that my life was only about surviving, digging myself out, one suffering moment to another. There had to be more to life than that.

An old friend from work contacted me and asked if I would like to arrange an appointment with a medical intuitive she was hosting at her home. I didn't know what a medical intuitive was, but I figured I had nothing to lose, if anything, it might be fun.

Weeks later when I arrived for my appointment, the intuitive, Brenda, handed me a clipboard with questions that I was instructed to answer. Sitting across from me, she too had a clipboard strategically raised so I couldn't see what she was writing. I dutifully completed the questions while she watched me and sketched on her paper. About five minutes had past, and she instructed me to set my clipboard aside.

"Illness can occur from unresolved emotions and negative thinking. Why do you not want to move forward with your life?" Brenda asked.

I looked at her, blank, "Haven't got a clue." *My muscular dystrophy happened because I think negatively? Ya, right. How could I do that, it's genetic. She's crazy.*

Why don't you want to grow up?

Again, blank, "Don't know?" I replied.

"You married your father.

I did what? I thought, but I didn't say anything.

"There's unexpressed anger in you," she said. She's just blurting this shit out. No explanation, just kind of throwing it out there.

I don't feel angry. I don't say this out loud, but I'm searching for anger and can't find it. *If you're looking for anger, then you should talk to my partner. He's the one with all the anger. It's like you're saying it's all my fault, I can't help it that all these things happened to me.*

"You have picked up patterns from your parents, and you behave the way you do because of those patterns. If you want to help your marriage, then you have to take a look at those patterns. Your children will do it too, just like you. You can stop it, though. If you identify the patterns in your life and make changes now, you can help prevent the patterns from being passed on."

"All of them?" I ask.

"Some patterns have already been passed on, and it will be up to your children to identify and change them, but from now on, you have the power to dissolve them."

"You have no pictures." There she goes again, just throwing things out there.

"What?"

"You have no pictures. You are not projecting anything into the future of what you want or look forward to. You're waiting to die."

I looked and scoured the dark recesses of my being, seeking a glimpse of my future. The only picture was of a decrepit, weak version of myself, slumped in a wheelchair. I quickly detached, breaking the visual link. I didn't want what was in my future. I would rather die. She was right. I was waiting to die.

"You can heal yourself, and you can heal the dysfunctional childhood patterns that have been passed on." I think of my children. I want that for them, and I'll do anything to make that happen. I found my currency for change.

"What do I have to do?"

My pilgrimage does not begin in Mecca, at the Golden Temple or the Western Wall. It commenced in a small cottage at the water's edge in Ontario where I packed all the courage I could muster, the bodily strength I could gather and remaining traces of a younger me, the plucky, challenge-loving Tomboy from Merritt Parkway. It was there that I began my travel inwards in search of something elusive but palatable, that had enough allure to keep me moving forward and sustenance to preserve my hope for a life of joy. There would be no planes to catch, luggage to carry or maps to read. My pilgrimage began right there, right then, by venturing into the black hole. My heart raced, sweat formed at the center of my back, and my muscles grew tense, making me weep and shaky at the thought of it, but I had no choice. To stay stagnant was suicidal, so I had to go up, forward or through the fear, trusting in something greater than myself to guide me.

I read every book I could get my hands on. *Relationship Rescue*, by Phil McGraw, *How to Heal Your Life*, by Louise Hay, *Real Magic*, by Wayne Dyer, *Conscious Loving*, by Guy and Kathleen Hendricks, *Anatomy of the Spirit*, by Caroline Myss and more. I devoured anything about creating positive change or identifying limiting beliefs highlighting key points and taking notes trying to satiate my inner hunger for peace. If they gave me an exercise, I did it. I wrote letters to my Mom, Dad, my partner and the kids expressing how I felt. I made lists of what I wanted. Expressed anger by screaming in a pillow and practiced forgiveness.

I typed positive statements on pieces of paper and posted them on the bathroom mirror, on the refrigerator, by my bed and on a card in my wallet and every time I saw the paper of affirmations I read them from top to bottom. I chose affirmations from the books I read or changed them, making sure they were relative to me and that when I said them, they made sense to me, rolling off my tongue with ease. I am lovable; I am healthy, strong and powerful; I am worthy just as I am; I am valuable; The Universe supports me.

I practiced repeating them in front of the mirror, holding my stare trying not to avert my eyes and repeated them to memory creating a personal mantra that I would say to myself in times of stress.

I began walking every day, for five minutes, barefoot in the grass. When I mastered five minutes, I walked for 10 minutes and then 15 minutes. Eventually, I put on water shoes because they were light and I could feel the ground beneath and walked the gravel road gradually increasing the distance.

I started swimming in the lake, staring at the clouds above and feeling the water touch my skin. I learned to meditate by concentrating on my breath.

I continued to read, practiced different types of meditation, exercised, tried to live the spiritual principles daily, and my life began to change. I stopped resisting my experience and started moving through it, opening myself to new possibilities.

A friend told me about a retreat called Hollyhock on Cortes Island in British Columbia where they offered a broad range of programming. I looked it up and discovered they had a visual arts class that summer about creating art from tapping into your inner self. I wanted to go, but it was on the other side of the country, and I thought I could not afford it, I couldn't do it by myself and my partner would never support it.

One night shortly after, with no warning or reason I bolted straight up in bed. The message came to me with no sound but with the clarity, I had never before known. I knew I had to go. I knew I had to do it.

Fear gripped me as I made the booking, my partner challenged me every day telling me it was selfish to take a trip alone, and I was frightened my body would not be capable of the journey. How would I ever manage two planes and two ferries all by myself?

The trip ended up being more about walking through my fears than about what program I chose because it challenged so many mental and physical limitations that I had created for myself. My accommodations were at the top of a hill accessible only by a walking path through the woods. Every day I traversed the tree roots and rocks to attend the programming and dining hall at the bottom of the hill building up my stamina and confidence with each pass. In one activity, we were blindfolded and led over the shoreline rocks by a partner to experience trust and to connect us with our other senses. It was terrifying and exhilarating all at the same time.

The universe supported my movement forward presenting opportunities for me to break perceived limits and to reconnect me with who I really was.

Those opportunities didn't always come in the form of holidays in British Columbia. Sometimes they came in displays of tears, anger, fear, frustration, judgment and anxiety. Every negative reaction was a clue that a limiting belief was active giving me the chance to be present with it, by allowing and observing it. I felt the anger, sensed it in my body, witnessed its effects and questioned what I believed to be true.

I felt I had the power within me to heal, and my body responded. Within months the pain subsided, sleep embraced me and energy surged through me and into what I did.

As a couple, we agreed to try again. Reconciling, we moved into the city into a new home, new school for the kids, new friends and a whole new outlook on life. I was excited about my future again.

SLIDING BACKWARD

A couple of years later, my physical mobility began to decline, noticeable by the physical tasks that I struggled to complete. Rising from the toilet or climbing the stairs became more arduous and I became derailed from my spiritual wave of excitement and expectation. I was doing everything I was supposed to be doing. I was thinking positively, I was using positive affirmations, I was visualizing what I wanted, I took care of my body, watched what I ate, I exercised and yet my muscles continued to deteriorate.

I felt myself emotionally, physically and mentally sliding backward into old ways of being. I meditated less and participated in activities that were not in my highest good such as drinking and smoking. Old habitual limiting beliefs began to surface again. "It doesn't matter what I do," "everything happens to me," and "what's the use?" I put so much energy and investment in my ability to heal myself that when my muscles continued to deteriorate it deflated me.

We installed a stair lift to help me get to and from the second floor, and I started using a walker to get around outside the home. Emotionally I felt like I was starting from scratch, grieving the life I wanted, the life I dreamed for myself and the person I wanted to be. The positive thinking stuff was a sham. It didn't work. I backslid into the familiar void.

Remnants of our struggling relationship from years before began to resurface too with increased distance, shallow conversation and partner's cutting sarcasm.

"You seem distant. Everything O.K.?" I'd ask.

"Ya, I'm fine," he would reply. I ignored my intuition telling me otherwise.

My partner surprised me on my 40th birthday with a four-day cruise to the Caribbean for just the two of us. I looked forward to spending some quality time together so we could have some long, deep conversations, intimate dinners and romantic evenings to recharge our marriage but I was nervous about the physical obstacles. The arrangements he made did not take into consideration my new physical limitations requiring me to rely on him to help me. It embarrassed me to know that I would have to ask him to help me get up stairs and to help me stand after sitting. I knew somewhere deep inside that my needs repulsed him too.

A couple of weeks later while sitting on the couch watching television with my partner, I leaned in to give him a gentle kiss. He pulled back and said, "I want a divorce. I can't handle you being disabled." Speechless and stunned, I pushed my body up from the couch slowly and awkwardly because of my weak muscles and tried to escape upstairs to distance myself from him. I struggled to comprehend what just happened, wanting to collapse somewhere and weep but I was trapped. My daughter was in my room because of her broken arm; I was in her room with a loft bed that I couldn't get into and a floor I wouldn't be able to get up from.

I fell into a swivel office chair, tried to process his cutting words as they tore through me like a funnel cloud, opening old wounds, leaving me feeling abandoned and discarded. There was nothing left of me but a shell, a lifeless body barely able to support its weight and incapable of recovering from the flood of loss, grief, abandonment and loneliness that surged from the inside up and out through my pores. It would not be suppressed any longer, and beckoned to be heard.

Days later I found myself lying on my back in bed, cocooned by the duvet covered mattress staring at the ceiling paralyzed by life.

I give up. I do not know how to recover. I keep bouncing back; I keep going on, moving forward but inevitably I end up in a state of chaos and suffering again. I am done. There is no rebound left inside of me.

I give up. I surrender. I surrender to a different way. I am letting go of the reins and letting the Universe take the lead. I will do whatever I am supposed to do. Just show me the way.

LETTING GO

Complete paralysis and devastation was what it took for me to give myself entirely over to the Universe. There was a simple knowing, a feeling, a gentle whisper in my heart that knew I would be O.K. and all I needed to do was trust. Trust that everything that was happening was in my best interest, that the Universe supported me and took care of me moment by moment. I needed to open myself up to a power greater than myself and relinquish my illusion of control.

At the time, I was a shadow of the powerful, vibrant Tomboy from Port Colborne, and my self-confidence and self-esteem were negligible. For the next two years, step by step I worked at being present, bringing awareness to my thinking and challenging my fears. Each step I reaffirmed my trust in the divine plan, my belief that everything was for me and that the Universe supported my every move forward as I strategically worked at patching the cracks in my foundation of perception. How did I do that? The key was cleaning up the childhood limiting beliefs that created the fear and unhappiness.

The question was, though, what were the limiting beliefs and where could I find them?

~⊙⌒~

CHAPTER TWO: CHILDHOOD

We were left to our own devices most of the time and on a good day, Vince's Dad, our neighbor wasn't home blocking the driveway with his car. All us kids could ride our bikes around in endless circles one behind the other. As a tomboy, I fit right in with the boys on the street, riding my big, red bike with the bar so that I had to swing my leg up and over the seat to get on. Out of the four of us, I was the youngest but relished in the fact that I stood a half foot taller than all of them. Growing up on a street full of boys made me care less for dolls and more for hockey sticks, but pride still existed in my girlishness. The four of us played from the time we got up, to the time the street lights came on, going inside only to use the bathroom or grab a bite to eat.

When at home, sometimes my brother John would play judo with me, throwing me over his back with the Ogoshi move or put me in a full Nelson headlock pretending to punch the crap out of me. That was the fun part. The not so much fun part was when he used CIA torture tactics. As he straddled me and pinned my shoulders to the ground with his knees, he would hang his head over mine and let his spit form, stretch and droop just above my mouth. That sent me into blood-curdling screams. He would suck it up at the last possible moment and laugh as he finished the torture session with endless tickling.

I guess John got bored too, and that meant he would bug me until I cried and even then, that didn't make him stop. When he pointed his forefinger an inch from between my eyes and drew it in and out rapidly, insistently, without escape, making an obnoxious sound like, "ouwh, ouwh, ouwh, it drove me crazy. I tried to ignore it, but he would persist, determined to get a reaction out of me. When I became hysterical, he'd relinquish the torment, and I'd go running to tell Mom, but no one ever did anything about it. She'd say, "stop it," in a not so caring, exhausted voice and keep puffing on her Cameos. Even Dad didn't do anything, so I just had to take it.

When John gave me noogies (head rubs with his knuckles), sat on me or called me Crudhead who lives in toilet land I still cried in the hopes that someone would stick up for me, but they never did. I knew Mom and Dad loved and cared about me, but it seemed they just didn't have the energy to deal with it, leaving me feeling vulnerable and unprotected. I can only guess that they were too exhausted from working all day, cooking and cleaning for four kids or, I was crying so hard and so often they just gave up.

Sometimes Dad would take me with him to do errands. We'd go grocery shopping, go to the bank or very rarely to Kentucky Fried Chicken when he had a "buy one bucket of chicken, get one free" coupon. Time with Dad was savored because working shift work meant he was usually sleeping when I was awake and working when I was asleep. I lapped up every second I had with him, and it didn't matter what we were doing. Even watching him spit and polish his leather holster belt was fun.

As soon as he came home, I'd follow him to his room, breathing in his presence and the security that enveloped me as I sat on the edge of his bed, watching as he unsnapped the black leather pouch and pulled out his gun. He would open up the barrel and tilt the revolver so the bullets would slide out quietly into his hand, placing them lightly in a dish on his dresser making them ding and roll towards the edges where they stopped. Next he'd unsnap the small, black pouch and remove the handcuffs, opening them up, securing the open ring through the trigger guard of the revolver and then, carefully closing the cuff until the light clicking sound stopped. After securing the gun, he'd unbuckle the shiny black belt and shoulder strap that seemed to unleash the gentle, fun-loving, family man I admired and loved so much, an entirely different persona from the intimidating, police officer present only moments before.

With his uniform neatly hung in the closet, he'd throw on an ironed, button down shirt and pants and head for the kitchen where he'd start preparing dinner.

"Come and get it or I'll throw it out!" Dad would bellow.

We knew he didn't mean it, but we would still run from all over our 5-bedroom house to our usual spots at the table. Dad sat at the end with my Mom to his left. John, eight years my senior slid in beside her and Shawn the oldest sat at the end opposite to my Dad. The two girls, Leone and I, sat on the wall side. Dinner was all about eating, talking and laughing. I don't remember ever having a serious conversation around that table. Things were pretty laid back, and nothing was better than listening to loud, mouth wide open, belly laughs from everyone at the table. I often felt alone except for these times when we were all together at the table, comforted by the intimacy, the melting butter on mashed potatoes and the physical presence of those I loved.

After dinner Mom would shoo us away, so she could drink coffee and smoke cigarettes with Dad in the living room. No wonder Mom wanted Dad all to herself because she got more love and respect from him than she ever got from her own family. He cared about what she thought and never once raised his voice to her. She didn't have to make any decisions, take care of the finances or concern herself with anything. Dad took care of her, and Mom thrived, laughing and smiling easily in his company.

Sometimes when bored I would scour the table next to the washing machine for change removed from pockets on washing day. If there were no coins there, the next best place to look would be in the top drawer of my brother's dresser. In their room in the basement, standing in between two twin beds, stood a five drawer dresser overlooked by mounted fish and hunting guns resting in their deer antler cradles on the wall. Inside that top drawer was a kitchen cereal bowl overflowing with quarters, dimes, nickels, and pennies which made it easy to take a few without anyone finding out. There was always a plethora of money in that dish because ever since John turned sixteen, Dad had made sure that both of them worked on the boats going through Great Lakes, shoveling coal or being deck hands over Christmas holidays.

With fifty cents in my pocket, I would head across Hwy 58 to the Jong's convenience store where I usually went to buy milk. They had a big, glass counter that you could look in from the top, front and both sides, containing all the penny candy like Double Bubble chewing gum, Mojos, caramels and pixie sticks. Standing there and deciding was so exhilarating, asking for one of those and two of these while the store owner stood patiently, gradually filling the little brown bag, keeping count of how much I spent. Gripping the edges of the counter swaying my body down and up and over, peering in with my nose inches from the glass I contemplated my choices, making sure I didn't miss something new.

The five and ten cent items sat on top of the counter right out there in the open. The owner, distracted by someone cashing out at the register, made it simple for me to gently grab a 10 cent candy bar and with a smooth retraction of my arm slide it nonchalantly into my coat pocket. It surprised me when the Dutch owner pointed to my pocket and asked me, "Show me your pocket?"

"What?"

"Show me your pocket?" He caught me. I reached in and slowly drew out the candy bar and placed it on the counter.

"Get out."

I made my way quickly to the door; head drooped and my stomach hanging below my knees. "I can't believe he caught me."

Rounding the corner to Oakwood public school ashamed and empty handed, I wondered why I had done that. I didn't need that extra candy with the fifty cents in my pocket, but I did it anyway. I didn't feel nervous or scared doing it, but felt rotten getting caught.

The next day, sitting in Mrs. Pelham's grade four class, the P.A. system came on, and the Oakwood School secretary spoke, "Please send Lori Brant down to the office please." All the kids in unison said," ahhhHHHHHHHhhhhh," meaning they thought I must be in trouble. I couldn't think of anything that I had done wrong, so I was not worried and enjoyed the momentary escape from class.

Once I arrived, Mr. Trist the Principal opened his office door, pointed to a chair opposite his desk and said, "Have a seat," and left, closing the door behind him. Sitting across from me in the Principal's chair was a tall, unfamiliar man wearing a suit and trench coat with the buttons undone at the front.

"Lori, I am a Detective with the Police Department and need to ask me a few questions." I was surely stuck in that chair feeling terrified that I'd done something wrong but didn't know what it was that I'd done.

"Did you steal candy from the Jong's convenience store?" he questioned.

"Yes."

"Did the owner ask you to leave and never return?"

Never return? Scouring my memory, I recalled only that the owner had asked me to put back the chocolate bar that was in my pocket, that he told me to leave, but I didn't remember him asking me never to come back. He didn't yell or anything, so I thought it was no big deal that he caught me trying to take that candy. It certainly wasn't a big enough deal to call a detective.

"I guess," I replied reluctantly.

"Where were you last night?" he asked.

"I went shopping with my parents at the Glenday Mall."

"What time did you leave?"

I didn't even know what I was so nervous about. Taking that candy didn't seem to have anything to do with going shopping last night. I figured it was something big that I must have done, given he was asking the questions so I lied anyway and said, "We left at 4:30 pm," knowing full well we could never leave at 4:30 pm because Mom never got home before 5:10 pm.

"Are you sure?" he questioned.

"Yes, I am sure."

"Did you call the Jong's convenience store and threaten to blow it up?"

My mouth dropped open, and my eyes went big and wide, "No!" I exclaimed.

"Someone called and said there was a bomb in the store. They thought it might be you."

"No, I'd never do something like that," I replied. "Like I said, I was with my Mom and Dad shopping."

"I'm going to be speaking with your parents, and I don't want you ever to step foot in that store again. Do you understand?"

"Yes, sir."

He nodded upwards toward the door and said, "You can go."

I used all my strength to rise from the chair. Sweating, my heart beating against my chest wall and with hands shaking, I began my slow walk back to Mrs. Pelham's class. It was hard to believe what had just transpired, that the police thought I was a bomber and they were going to tell my Dad, the Sergeant of the OPP, that they thought I was going to blow up the Jongs. "I'm dead," I thought. This was big, and I knew I was going to get it this time.

It was the longest day ever and when that bell rang my heart sank and my mouth was dry just thinking about what was going to happen when I got home. Inching my way along the highway and rounding the corner of Merritt Parkway, I could see my 6 foot, 2-inch father puttering around in the garage. It was making it hard for me to breathe just thinking about how embarrassing this would be for him being the sergeant and all. Head down, feet dragging I turned in the driveway, Dad looked at me and shockingly, acted as if nothing was wrong. "Hi Pumpkin, how was your day?" he asked. Was it possible? Did the Detective not call him?

Practically laughing with relief, comforted and grateful for my luck, I replied, "Good," and I headed in for a snack.

The next day after returning home from school, Dad instructed me to have a seat in the living room. Turned out my luck had run short, the Detective had called him, and I braced myself for the onslaught. I had it coming, and I knew it. The look of disappointment in my father's eyes that day was worse than any spanking or scolding. Letting him down made me feel sick to my stomach and I ached to escape his gaze. I just cried with the intensity of a dam being blown wide open, letting go of all my anxiety, shame and embarrassment I felt since I got called down to the office. Dad was contemplating my punishment while he sat there, quiet, solemn and detached.

"Your mother and I agree, you will no longer be having a birthday party. You'll have to tell your friends it's canceled."

He knew I had spent weeks planning my party, all the games I would play, the prizes we'd give out and had already hand delivered the matching invitations to my friends at school. How would I ever get the courage to tell them all that it was canceled? They would surely ask why and I could never tell them the truth: that it was because the police thought I was a bomber and a thief.

Collapsing, spread out on the couch, I wailed "No, please don't, don't, not my party!" Pulling out all the dramatic flair I could muster, crying and sobbing till the snot ran in my mouth, and my shirt was wet from tears, I begged, pleaded, cried, and sobbed while slithering down the cushions until I hit the floor. Devastated with shame, guilt and regret, I kept trying to hit just the right place, a place where Dad would feel sorry for me, give in and change his mind.

"I promise, I will never do it again, ground me forever or make me clean the house, anything else, but please don't force me to cancel the party."

This went on for a long time, and I wasn't even sure I could keep it up until finally he interrupted my hysterics and said, "Alright, you can have your party, but you won't be getting a birthday present from your Mom and me."

Running over to my Dad sitting in his red, velvet chair, I dropped to my knees and wrapped my arms around him, thanking him from the bottom of my soul.

"Thank you, thank you, thank you!"

Mom sure won't be happy when she finds out Dad softened and changed my punishment, I thought.

It turned out Dad's punishment had the sting it was intended to have because even though I still got to hang donuts from the ceiling and bob for apples at my party, I just didn't feel the joy that came with being the birthday girl. Besides Mom and Dad's gift, their special look, smiles, and pride were missing too, and it was more than noticeable. They both stayed upstairs the whole time and didn't even come down to watch me open gifts.

Nothing is better than showing your parents something special you've done, something special you got because parents care about everything you do, as no one else. "Mom, Dad, Look at me! Mom, Dad, watch me!" In fact, parents care about everything, even if you go number two each day. Who else cares about that? Disappointing and embarrassing Dad the way I did, changed me, leaving me open, as though my badness was visible for everyone to see, making me feel sick inside, and I didn't like it.

The birthday party didn't turn out the way I wanted. Everyone had a good time, but I felt hollow inside. I had never really had to do anything to make Mom and Dad proud of me before because it just seemed I could do no wrong. I was perfect in their eyes, but now, it was different. There was a wedge between what I wanted them to feel about me and what I thought they felt about me, and I put it there. I wanted things to go back to the way they were so I could feel loved again.

September of 1978 was approaching with the excitement of attending McKay Senior Public. Attending school with the grade seven and eight students from the west side of the city was overshadowed by reports that Cara and Sandra were waiting for our arrival so they could beat Lisa and me up. We were perplexed because we didn't even know who those two kids were. As the first day approached, the threat became worse as both of us were getting crank calls and rumors were circulating about us getting our faces bashed in. I told Dad I was scared and didn't want to go to McKay Senior anymore.

He asked me why, and I reported to him everything that had transpired over the summer and how they said they couldn't wait for us to get there on the first day so they could do us in. Intimidated and terrified, I spurted out the story, declaring that it was sure suicide to show up at McKay Senior and that they should consider an alternate school for both of us. Dad sat there in the red velvet chair, his elbow resting on the arm with his hand holding up his head, cradled between the thumb and forefinger, listening and taking it all in but not saying anything.

The situation seemed unbearable, so that night before our first day, Lisa and I were strategizing our survival when I got a telephone call.

"Hello," I said.

"Hi, it's Cara. I just wanted to say I am sorry for all the crank calls and saying I was going to beat you up. I hope we can be friends."

Jaw dropping shock paralyzed my body, and I couldn't say anything back into the phone as my mind searched her statement for sarcasm or trickery. With none found, I contemplated the possibility of a friendly truce. Both seemed implausible and without hardly taking a breath, I blurted out, "Sure."

"Bye, "she said.

"Bye," I replied.

Moments later, still stunned, I got a second call, the same as the first from Sandra apologizing and wanting to be friends. On one hand, I was relieved that the bullying would stop but on the other, I felt like I was being manipulated and tricked. Needing confirmation, Lisa and I informed my parents about the phone calls and questioned their sincerity. They agreed that they must have had a change of heart. I loved the way Dad always made me feel safe, secure and took care of me. He didn't say anything, but I figured he must have had something to do with their sudden change of attitude. I imagine him showing up in their driveway in a cruiser, stepping out and knocking on the door in full uniform terrifying them without having to say a word.

DAD

I continued to excel in sports and was thrilled that I was chosen to play Dorothy in the school play, "The Wizard of Oz." Rehearsals began in September and between the play and after school sports teams, my spare time was limited, and I loved it.

Tuesday morning, April 17, 1979, I was getting ready for school like any other day, when Mom asked, "Can you stay home and keep an eye on your Dad?" Apparently, he was not feeling well and as always Mom never missed a day of work no matter what. I couldn't believe my luck. How awesome is that, to be able to stay home from school and watch TV? Before finishing my call to Sheila explaining my proposed absence, Mom turned around and said, "No, you go on, I will stay with your Dad."

When I returned home from play practice, I found out Dad was in the hospital again. This time though, he had an aneurysm and they sent him to Hamilton, an hour away. Mom was a mess and kept her distance from me, talking to Lyle, my Dad's best friend, in the kitchen while smoking her Cameos. I went off into my room, saddened at the thought that he was sick but comforted that everything would be O.K. since things always had a way of working themselves out.

No one shared much with me over the next couple of days with regards to Dad's health or how he was doing, and I took that as meaning he must be doing fine. What seemed to be more important was deciding whether or not they should cancel my brother Shawn's wedding. The hall was paid for, people were coming in from all over Ontario, and they were not even sure they could get hold of everyone to tell them not to come, given the wedding was only three days away.

Someone must have decided that it was a "go" because I found myself sitting in a beauty salon chair that Saturday getting my hair done with my sister Leone. It seemed odd that the stylist covered both our heads with rollers since our hair was already very curly. It was all the rage to get your hair permed so that you'd have flowing, long ringlets or big waves like Farah Fawcett but it never turned out that way. Instead, you'd end up looking like Shirley Temple or have an afro like Diana Ross. It didn't matter anyway, since John showed up to say, "We have to go to Hamilton right now, let's go."

Leone and I helped to undo all those rollers, whipped off our capes and ran through the mall to the car. The reason for the urgency escaped me as we headed towards Hamilton the day of Shawn's wedding. There was a frenzy of activity, and I was swept up in it like a fallen leaf floating in the river's strong moving current, just going along with it, void of emotional attachment to any part of it or appreciation of any potential dangers ahead.

Outside Dad's hospital room family members coached me on what to say.

"Say something positive," said Leone.

"Say something that will make him feel good," said John.

I tossed around a few ideas in my head until the door opened and I entered, finding a place at the foot of his hospital bed. He was lying there, eyes closed with a thick tube clogging up the opening to his mouth, looking placid and pale as the antiseptic aroma penetrated my nostrils and taste buds.

Contemplating what it was that I should do, I yearned to sing "Somewhere Over the Rainbow," to him. I had practiced it over and over a million times in the living room while Mom and Dad were reading their newspapers after dinner. They never complained, but I could see them hiding their laughter behind their Toronto Star probably thinking, "Oh God, here she goes again." Questioning that it might be too loud and disturb other patients, I chewed my inner lip, wavering between my aching to sing and the pressure to behave properly. Inching over near his bedside, sliding my hand onto his and tucking my fingers in near his palm, I blurted, "Come on Dad, you have to get better. Who is going to practice pitching with me if you are not going to?" It felt awkward and empty but, that's what came out. Dad's grip tightened around my tiny fingers, and I knew he felt my love, regardless of my odd remark and not hearing my song.

If there was anything I could go back and change it would be that moment. If only the words that came out were, "I love you Dad, more than anything in this whole world. You were the best Dad anyone could ever want, and I loved every single moment I had with you. I hope I made you proud. I miss you so much. You made me feel safe and protected. I love your laugh, your wisdom. I dream of you walking me down the aisle and holding my babies. I look forward to the opportunity to sit with you as an adult and discuss life, my choices and my plans."

Shawn and Rosemary got married, and the celebration went on with an undercurrent of concern that penetrated the reception. Small groups of my parents' worried friends rallied around Mom and our family, trying unsuccessfully to celebrate the new union and sympathize with Dad's declining health at the same time. The dire situation was still lost on me acknowledging that yes, Dad was sick but not sick enough to stop the festivities, and I still believed that everything would restore to what was familiar and predictable.

Sunday following the wedding, rehearsals for, "The Wizard of Oz," continued, as final touches were added and actors were readied for their first performance. I was feeling sad, beginning to sense the cloud of concern that hung in the air at home. My family was trying to distract me and keep me away from the stress and chaos hovering around them, but it left me feeling isolated and detached from what was going on.

My mood must have drawn attention to me as I sat in the theater seat waiting for my scene on stage because kids began to gather around me. I enjoyed the attention.

When I was urged to disclose the reason for my tears, I began sharing the details of Dad's hospitalization with my friends. "He has been in the hospital since last week, and we had to rush up there the day of Shawn's wedding." Shock and pity appeared on my friend's faces. They seemed to be more worried than my family was. Figuring I must have exaggerated and embellished the story too much because of their strong reaction, I began to reassure them, "It's O.K., it is no big deal. He will be alright."

It was school as usual Monday and the "Wizard of Oz," rehearsal after that. The first matinee was only days away and after eight months of practice, we were excited about finally performing. In a sea of actors and dancers, I spotted my friend's Dad approaching me, and my eyes stayed on him. His presence seemed peculiar and his direction even more so. "Lori, your Mom asked me to come and get you."

Immediately upon my arrival at home, Mom, Leone, Shawn, John and I climbed into the station wagon and headed to Hamilton. Dad had made a turn for the worse, and we were going to cheer him up again.

The mood was solemn, as we walked silently through the halls toward my father's room. Mom went inside with my older brother Shawn, to see Dad and speak with the doctor. Standing there waiting for direction, a nurse approached and whispered, "O.K. you can go in now." Entering, I noticed Mom standing back near the wall, weeping and distraught and Dad lying motionless, sicker than he was on our previous visit. I placed my hand in his, hoping for the gentle grasp that would reassure me he was in there, healing, and on his way back to me but there was no response. His hand, limp and weighted, made no gesture or connection.

"We should let him get some rest now," the nurse said, as she gently guided us out the door and into a small windowless room with a little table off to the side and four chairs. Once seated, I realized there was only John there with the nurse and me.

I must have been foggy in my head because John said something and what I thought he said was, "Dad is dying." I broke down into inconsolable sobs, the way I usually did when something big happened. *Did he really say Dad was dying or did I misunderstand him? Maybe he didn't.* Still bellowing, crying and grasping for new air to cry harder and louder, I contemplated about how I could find out what he had said. I would feel stupid asking now since I was crying so dramatically and all, that I decided to keep on crying in case that was what he said. I guess my bawling was too much for everyone, so the nurse told me to quiet down as not to disrupt the patients. I didn't care. If I did hear him correctly, I had the right to cry as loud and as long as I wanted.

"You're lucky, you're Dad has lived a long time. Not like the sixteen-year-old down the hall who is dying," the nurse said.

The confirmation landed hard. It was real. My sobbing intensified. He was dying.

"I don't care about the girl down the hall!"

I watched my cousin Tannace put her mascara on as she looked into my dresser mirror. Releasing the brush from its container, pulling on the bristles to clear the excess and raising it to her lashes, she applied the makeup with gentle strokes. Her mouth was open as she leaned in towards the mirror to get a better view caressing both the lower and the upper lashes with the brush. Pulling her shoulders back, satisfied, she replaced the applicator into its sleeve and twisted it closed. She reached for the steaming hot curling iron and twisted a section of her hair up in it. She held it there, still looking in the mirror and then would touch the trapped burning hair to see if it was done, releasing it with the press of the button. Twist and curl and release.

Dad is dead.

Twist and curl and release.

My life has changed forever and yet other people; their lives just go on as usual, untouched, unaltered.

Twist and curl and release.

This death is mine, and no one understands what it's like to be me. I am alone, standing outside looking in.

Twist and curl and release.

The flowers surrounded the casket, flowing out along the walls, cradling it on three sides. Half the casket remained closed, with the upper half opened, exposing the silky, padded white lining. Inside, fully clothed, lying in his police uniform was Dad. I knew it was Dad but at the same time, knew it was not Dad. This body, lying in front of me was chalky, white and absent of character. I didn't give much thought to those little lines around his eyes or his mouth in everyday life yet that was where life rested. In the tiny folds of his pink colored skin, he shared the essence of who he was. I felt the expectation to cry, to kiss him, to touch him, but I didn't. He was not real. I felt no loss as I stood before his casket. The real loss was felt when I imagined him in my mind, laughing, sparkling, radiating, loving, listening, living. I slid past the head of the casket and fell in behind the rest of my family.

We all loaded in the funeral car, slowly exiting the garage behind the hearse. White-gloved, saluting officers and shiny, polished cruisers blocked the cars from breaking into our line. We pulled up to the empty spots outside the church and watched the six police officers open the hearse door and robotically remove the casket from its womb, grab hold of the side rails and carry Dad up and into the church double doors. People were scattered on the sidewalks, the lawn and behind barricades on the street, looking on as we exited the vehicle and walked dutifully and quietly in and through the same double doors.

Hundreds of officers took up all of the seats on the left side while the right was filled with family and friends. There was not enough room to hold everyone, leaving well-wishers standing along the sides in the back and outside. Someone was holding my hand as we walked up the middle behind the pallbearers as they positioned the casket in its resting place. Front center, the cherry wood peeked out from under the cascading flowers hugging its surface as my family took their seat in the first pew on the right. My senses were full as I took in everything. The people, flowers, music, and the words crowded together.

The thickness of emotion and the stillness of time permeated the air. Images played in my head of the open casket. I felt the way he looked.

We filed out first, down the middle aisle and back out to the funeral car, pulling away first as hundreds of cars followed. Looking out the window, the Tinman, Scarecrow, and the Lion stood on the corner watching me, and I slowly lifted my hand gesturing a hello, taking in their appearance and feeling the support. Barricades, flashing police car lights, white gloves, families going to the grocery store and people pumping gas. Ordinary mundane tasks continued to be performed by all those untouched. In my inner circle time stopped, but outside, life was being lived. I wanted them to stop what they were doing to steady me, to wait for me, to help bear some of the weight but they just kept going.

I couldn't help but feel a sense of pride as the funeral procession led by officers on motorcycles inched its way through our small town blocking intersections like a parade. Everyone who had come in contact with my Dad loved him, and his funeral was a tribute to that.

At the Oakwood Cemetery, our family moved to the side of the casket as the pallbearers placed it over the grave. I can't remember anything else that happened that day. I think my mind was so filled up it stopped letting more things in.

The next day, my Mom said, "Lori, I think you should do your play. It's what your Dad would have wanted."

I called Miss. Shoxie and asked if it was OK if I did the play that night and she was excited that I was up for it.

I was not prepared, and felt a little anxious about remembering everything I had to bring. My costume, shoes, pantyhose, hair ribbons and socks. It was awkward when I arrived because everyone was looking at me and not talking, so I just spoke up and started telling them about the funeral and all the police officers and how they were blocking the roads and stuff.

"How can you talk about it like that, like it was nothing?" someone asked.

"Because I was proud of him," I replied.

And that was it. I melted into everyone's excitement about the show, and I was just Lori, playing Dorothy in the Wizard of Oz and nothing else. It felt good, like the burden was lifted and I could breathe. I did my best that night, singing my heart out and not forgetting a single line. It wasn't until the final scene when Dorothy was being brought home by the Oz that I was unclear of the stage direction. Miss. Shoxie in the Orchestra pit was just smiling and directed me into the basket of the hot air balloon, so I got in. Suddenly, the balloon started rising and into the rafters with just me and the OZ holding on to the ropes. I felt so good at that moment, knowing I had done it. I wished that balloon would just keep on going up so I could hold onto that feeling and not have to come back down and deal with death, sadness, and the hollow feeling deep inside.

Now, looking back, it is hard to believe that I did that play the day after Dad's funeral but in a way, that was what I knew. That was what happened. People just go on doing their stuff. They buy their groceries, get gas, get married, go to school, curl their hair and put on mascara.

I wish someone had been honest with me early on and told me that Dad was going to die, but can only trust that he heard me whether the song was sung or not. I did write a poem, and when I showed Mom, she liked it so much she made a plaque and put it in the ground behind Dad's tombstone.

MOM

My Mom pretty much died right along beside Dad that day. She never moved from her paisley chair in the living room where she stared at the oil portrait of him in uniform, now drinking rye and cokes instead of coffee. She never missed a day of work, but when she got home, she would smoke cigarette after cigarette and drink after drink, curled up inside herself, trying to live life without Dad. I missed her laugh and smile.

Mom was delicate, weak and unavailable so I made sure not to talk to her about anything that might upset her. That meant I didn't get to grieve Dad's death because she couldn't handle it. My whole life changed after that. We went from not locking our doors to having bars installed on the windows and deadbolts on the doors. It took me a while to get used to bringing a key with me, and I was locked out more than once after school, having to wait until 5:10 pm when Mom came home from work to get inside.

I got talented at lying too, to avoid getting her hysterical over her new responsibility of raising me alone. She would say to her friends, "I am going to live long enough to see Lori finish school and then I am going to be with Lloyd." Not only did I have to deal with losing Dad, but I was dealing with Mom's quest for death too.

"I'm going to send you to reform school," she'd say, and I would just roll my eyes. She was annoying. What more did she want from me?

"You are lucky you have me as your daughter. I go to school, never skip, get A's and B's, do my homework, study. I could be a drug addict, or skip school or be failing!" It was irritating watching her crumble during the slightest of disagreements. Her grief consumed her. Dad was everything to her and her everything was gone.

I spent most of my time out of the house and figured out how to placate Mom and still do whatever I wanted.

Going to high school was exciting, and I looked forward to it all summer. I spent many days soaking up the rays at Nickel Beach on the shores of Lake Erie. The beach was all about getting an amazing tan, looking good, and drinking till we felt a buzz. My high school years were spent partying every weekend, getting drunk and smoking cigarettes while mom was oblivious, sitting in her chair smoking Cameos and drinking more rye than coke.

Samantha and I had just got back from spending March break at her parents' mobile home in West Palm Beach. Arriving home, I found the house empty and a handwritten note on the kitchen table. Mom's friend Helen wanted me to give her a call, so I did. Not long after, she rapped on the front door and let herself in.

"Hi."

"Hi Helen, what's up?" I asked.

"Lori, I have some bad news."

"What is it?"

"It's your Mom... She is in the hospital.... She has cancer... It doesn't look good."

I had my back to the kitchen counter, in front of the dishwasher and I slid down, dropping to the floor, hanging my head in my hands at my knees. "It's not fair," I screamed. "Dad died and now Mom, why me? It's not fair!" I felt distressed and overwhelmed as my mind raced with images of a gloomy future. Picking up the phone, I called Samantha, "My Mom has cancer and she is dying."

"I'll be right over," she said.

Samantha came and heard me: heard my pain, saw my distress but couldn't do anything. I wanted more from her, to make me feel better but her efforts seemed empty. I was truly alone.

Mom was understandably distraught, but even the Rye and Cokes couldn't put a smile on her face. She smoked and drank, smoked and drank. Friends came over, and she shared her pain and suffering. She liked the attention and enjoyed having people do things for her. I found comfort in my schedule, friends and ignored what was going on at home until summer came.

It was the first week of Grade thirteen, and I was sitting in Dad's red, swirly chair waiting for Samantha to pick me up. Mom was across from me holding an unlit cigarette, wearing her old quilted, pink housecoat not saying a word. I felt her fragility sitting there, drugged, eyes vacant, sad and lonely. *Mom, I love you. You did a good job raising me. I am going to go to University, get a good job, and take care of myself. You don't have to worry about me. I wish you weren't dying. I'll miss you. Is there anything you want to tell me? Any words of advice?* I think it, but I say nothing.

"Honk!" Samantha's here.

I grabbed my bag, headed for the door and yelled, "Bye."

Returning home, I climbed the stairs and was surprised not to see Mom sitting in her chair but lying on the couch, eyes closed and very still.

"Is she O.K?" I asked Leone.

"She's been like this all day."

We knew it was coming, but nothing prepares you for it. We took her to the hospital, but there was nothing they could do for her so, we decided to bring her home. A hospital bed replaced her Queen bedroom set, and a chair for the nurse replaced her nightstand. We wanted her to be at home, surrounded by her family, and familiarity of her things. Leone and I were relieved to relinquish responsibility to the nurse, leaving us to stand vigil as we watched cancer engulf our mother. We cringed at the sight of her grayish skin, sunken eyes and cheeks, as we took turns waiting for her to claim her next inhale. We knew death was calling, as long, silent breaks replaced her steady breath.

I held her limp hand, not wanting to miss another moment to share my feelings and began singing, "Somewhere over the

Rainbow," to her. The song was for Dad and her. To say I love you and to give them a part of me to take with them.

"If happy little bluebirds fly... beyond the rainbow... why ooh why..." I couldn't finish. The song was caught in my throat, blocked out by the tears and the pain surging from my heart.

The nurse saw me struggling and finished the song by softly singing, "Can't I?" I wanted to feel the squeeze of her hand in mine to let me know she heard it, that she knew I loved her, but there was no response.

"Hey everybody, I made some soup. Why don't you all have a bowl while it's hot," the relief worker from March of Dimes said. We left Mom with the nurse and sat down in the swirly chairs in the kitchen to have our meal. It was quiet. Not like the loud, enjoyable dinners we usually had when we were all together. I ate my soup. I didn't want to talk because the only topic hanging in the air was Mom dying, and I was done having the conversation. It just made me more depressed, and I was tired of being sad. I had all the grief from Dad dying and all the grief from Mom dying all squashed together, and I didn't want to open that door because I thought I might never get it closed. Right now, the only thing I wanted to do was eat soup.

The nurse poked her head in through the doorway and asked, "Can you all please come here for a minute?"

As we entered the room vacant of labored breath, we knew she was gone. She left the only time one of us wasn't with her. Mom slipped away into my father's arms, as her children gathered together over a bowl of soup in the next room.

I waited for tears to come, but they didn't. I was relieved. Relieved that her suffering had ended, and our waiting for her inevitable passing was over. Like the eye of a hurricane, everything was still and I waited, expecting the wrath of the second pass.

I was standing in the hallway as the paramedics came in to retrieve her body. They moved her onto the stretcher and then, there, right in front of all of us, the paramedic sealed her in a plastic bag with a "zzz zzz zip," enclosing Mom inside.

I can't believe they just did that.

I shouldn't have seen that.

I'm eighteen, an adult. I don't feel eighteen; I feel like I'm five. I just want to be five.

I hate growing up. I hate life. I hate God. I hate myself. I hate happy people.

We knew what we had to do. Funeral arrangements, phone calls, flowers, visitation. Shawn, the oldest was taking charge of the details and Leone and I found ourselves driving to the Niagara Square Mall.

"I can't believe Mom died, and we're going shopping for a dress," I said.

"I know. It feels weird but good at the same time," Leone replied.

"Ya, I know what you mean. It is kind of a relief to be doing something normal for a change, to be out of the house and away from all that."

"I can't believe they just zipped her up like that in the bag," my sister said.

"I can't believe they did it in front of us," I replied.

"Me neither."

I was one of those people going about my day, just like any other day but I was hollow on the inside, and my actions felt robotic. I was shopping, but I didn't care about the dress, didn't want to try anything on but knew I had to get one. I was out of the house, but death followed me.

I understood that the whole visitation thing could be comforting, to know that people cared enough to show their respect, but I longed for the days of childhood when I could fade into the background and excused from these responsibilities.

It was easier the second time, as I fell into line behind Shawn to view the open casket. The bottom half was closed, the top was open, and the same, puffy, pillow, satin lining upholstery hugged the sides. Mom's hair was set, and she wore a white dress with an accordion style collar framing her face. Her chalk complexion and fake lips were that of a stranger.

"She looks like Eileen Kanyo," Shawn whispered. I looked at Mom from this new perspective, thinking of Eileen, Mom's friend.

I stifled my laugh, and whispered back, "You're right, she does."

I didn't kiss her or touch her. It was Mom, but it was not Mom. I fell in behind Shawn as we passed the head of the casket and headed for the limousine.

Another funeral.

I felt detached. The experience was an extension of me, but I was separate from it too. It reminded me of Mom when she was signing her will.

She was sitting in her red, paisley chair reviewing the document with her lawyer who was trying to comfort her and get the legal business taken care of too. I was in the kitchen with Leone making lunch, taking breaks to peer around the corner at what was going on. She was shaking all over, making it difficult for her to hold the paper. Curled in on herself, alone and terrified at the finality of it all she couldn't bring herself to sign. I couldn't go to her. I thought about it. I imagined myself going over, wrapping my arms around her, supporting and loving her through the transition, but I didn't. It wasn't our way. We never hugged. We never said we loved each other or touched one another. I loved her, I wanted to be there for her, and it was in me to be loving and nurturing, but the relationship did not support it. Like it was unnatural. Our way was to do it alone even though we were surrounded by people who cared.

My brothers and sister were all married and had someone. They were paired up, leaning on each other. I had no one, and it felt like I did not belong. As we pulled into our spot behind the hearse at the church, I watched as pallbearers pulled out the casket, respectfully escorting it through the same double doors of the church that Dad had been carried through only five years earlier.

I found my mind flashing back to his funeral, comparing the two, finding the similarities both in appearance and ritual but mostly in its smothering sadness. I was tired of crying. Tired of grieving. I kept my distance, shutting down my heart, focusing on the end of the purple, cotton belt lying in my lap as I sat in the front pew with the rest of my family. Mom got what she wanted. She's with Dad, just like she said she'd be.

There were no police escorts, barriers or flashing lights but the procession, destination, and my movements were all the same.

"Can you turn that up?" John asked the driver.

"Pardon?"

"Can you turn the radio up?" he asked again. *The radio, you're listening to the radio?* I thought.

The driver obliged, and suddenly the melody registered in John's eyes as the notes of "Somewhere over the Rainbow," flowed from the limousine's speakers.

It's Mom.

She's O.K.

Mom's looking out for us.

Back at the house on Merritt Parkway, I felt displaced. The ceremonial traditions I had hated earlier in the week were a much-desired distraction for me now as I struggled to find my place. I was an outsider, standing on the sidelines as my siblings entertained their friends in the living room, finding comfort in their history and familiarity. There was no one for me. I wandered from my bedroom to the kitchen, to the living room not knowing where I belonged.

"Ding-dong."

Opening the front door, I see Ben, my boyfriend standing there. He's nervous, but his compassion is visible on his soft-ened face.

"Hi," he said.

"Hi," I reply.

I want him to leave. No one understands what it's like to be me and his attempts to comfort me will fail. Maybe that's why I feel detached. Maybe I've been expecting it, preparing for it, given she said she would only be here until I finished high school and then would go be with Dad. She was true to her word.

"I can't do this right now." I shut the door and went to my room alone.

My siblings had lives they needed to get back to, families to feed, wives to support and jobs to work at.

"Why don't you come live with us," Leone suggested.

"I'd rather stay here and finish school. Be near my friends.

"Are you sure, we'd love to have you."

"I'm sure, thanks."

They all left together. John and Leone were off to Toronto, and Shawn was going back to Niagara Falls. I stood at the top of the stairs, alone, in the now empty house. The silence filled the air as I turned around and took in the kitchen... then the hallway...then the living room. I envisioned mom sitting in her red, paisley chair with her ashtray to the right and coffee with milk and a teaspoon of sugar on the left. Across from her, I imagined Dad sitting in the red, swirly chair, legs stretched out and crossed at the ankles, holding the Toronto Star with two hands, the top left corner folded back so he could see Mom.

I saw flashes of Christmas, shiny silver tinsel dangling from the tips of the tree, family dinners in the dining room with Mom's crystal and English Rose china, apple pie, and stuffing. I saw Dad, John and Shawn outstretched on the gold carpet moaning, "Ohhhh I ate too much." I heard laughter.

I imagined Mom coming in the front door at 5:10, "I'm home!" she would say. "Come and get it or I'll throw it out!" Dad would yell. But no one came. The hum of the furnace. The creak of a floorboard. My chest rose and fell, my heart throbbed, and tears blurred my vision as gloom descended like a fog and hung in the air. There was the death of loved ones, death of voices, connection, comfort, and love. There was nothing left but me.

We sold our house at fourteen Merritt Parkway with the swirly black felt wallpaper in the living room, purple shag carpet in my bedroom and racing stripes in the basement, to David Burger's mother from next door. I found an apartment above a flower store on King Street in Port Colborne and took the red paisley furniture with me. I had missed too much school to catch up, so I decided to start fresh in January with a new semester.

"Wanna come with my family and me to Christmas Eve Mass?" Marsha asked three months later. She went to the same Church that I did, so I thought it might be good for me to have a place to go rather than sitting in my apartment alone, so I agreed.

We sat and waited for the service to begin, and I watched the parents with their children sharing special moments, their white leotards, shiny black shoes, men in suits and mothers in dresses. I yearned for connection, someone to belong to. *God, why did you take them both? What did I do wrong?* There were no answers and tears streamed down my face uncontrollably. *Oh God, not again.* They would not stop. I lowered my head making my hair fall forward to hide my embarrassment and sobbing face. My nose began to run, and I struggled to muffle the "snuff," sound as I attempted to halt my cries, but it was impossible. I rose from the pew, walked swiftly to the door with my head down, watched the tears drip from my cheeks to the floor, as I exited quickly through the double doors. The snow crunched under my feet and sobs released themselves from deep inside as I walked home. I just wanted to ignore Christmas. Ignore everything.

I went through all the stages of the grieving process before she died and then found myself going through it all again as I sat in the gold recliner, drinking Diet Coke, smoking cigarettes and watching TV. I could tell what stage I was in. Definitely depression. I had been sitting there for hours, alone think-ing. *If I died right now, I wonder how long it would take for someone to notice.* I tried to imagine reasons why someone might come to the door and the only one I could think of was that my rent was late.

I was scared. The shadows were dancing outside my window creating images of people, and I feared that someone was on the roof. *They can't be up there; I am just imagining things. What does it matter anyway? If they killed me, no one would care.*

The smoke dried my mouth, and I was no longer enjoy-ing the sensation but kept smoking anyway. My ashtray was full, and my Diet Coke was warm. I didn't feel like moving, but I forced myself up, got a cold one, snapped back the tab and released a "sheeeee." I took a sip, but my mouth still felt dry. *How long have I been sitting here? Has it been three days? Or two?* I didn't feel like showering, or going anywhere, but I was tired of sitting there, tired of being sad and lonely. *I am sick of having to deal with this shit.*

I could kill myself. How would I do it? People cut themselves, but I don't think I could do that. I could take pills, but I don't have any except aspirin, and I don't think I can kill myself with aspirin. Knowing my luck, I wouldn't kill myself but damage my organs creating more problems and things to deal with.

God, smoking's gross.

Who am I kidding? I can't kill myself.

I felt bad drawing someone in, bringing them down and ruining their day but I needed help. I needed someone who could handle what I was thinking, the death and the depression without worrying about scaring them.

"Hello," the voice said.

"Hello, this is Lori Brant, from the Church and I was wondering if I could speak to the Reverend."

"This is he."

"Hi, Reverend. I am sorry to bother you, but I am having a hard time dealing with my Mom's death, and everything and I can't seem to get myself out of it. I was wondering if you could help me?"

"Sure Lori. Where are you?"

"I'm at my apartment above the flower store downtown on Clarence."

"Where's your brother? Doesn't he live nearby?"

"He lives in Niagara Falls."

"Do you have his number? Do you mind giving it to me?"

"No." So I give it to him.

"Would it be O.K. for me to come by in an hour?"

"Yes."

"See you in an hour, Lori."

"O.K., Thanks. Bye."

I heard a knock and answered the door, surprised to see the Reverend and Shawn standing there. I feel my face grow warm and a bit awkward as I invite them in.

"Can I get you anything?"

"Got any wine?" the Reverend asks. I'm a bit surprised that he asks for wine since I am underage, but I have a bottle and pour him and Shawn a drink. We ended up just talking about regular stuff, and neither of them mentioned the reason for my call. I didn't tell them that I was so sad and lonely I wanted to kill myself. I didn't say that I didn't think anyone cared about me and that I could not stop smoking, drinking diet coke and having depressing thoughts. They stayed for a couple of hours until the bottle was empty and the Reverend began slurring his words. Shawn got up and said, "Well, I think I should be getting back home. So, you're good Lori?"

"Ya, I'm fine. Sorry for bothering you."

"No bother Lori, call me anytime," Shawn said.

I watched them descend the stairs and walk out into the night. I wished that Dad was there. He always made me feel better, and he took care of things. Other people tried to help, they distracted me, but the ache was always there. I wanted to feel the satisfaction of a long, slow, deep breath. That's how

Dad made me feel. Breathing and everything else seemed shallow and empty.

I tucked my sadness away deep in the corners of my being, put on a smile, pretended I was happy and continued to do it until I started to believe it.

ॐ

CHAPTER THREE:
DETECTING BELIEF PATTERNS

BELIEF PATTERNS

A belief is a thought with emotion(s) attached to it. Belief patterns form when we interpret what we experience and file it away in our memory like files in a filing cabinet. As we decode more and more experiences, our mind creates files by bunching similar experiences together finding generalities and commonalities amongst them. These files make up our subconscious or unconscious mind, a culmination of general ways to respond to similar situations or the foundation of our perception. Some are helpful like, "look both ways before you cross the street," don't lick a frozen pole," or "don't eat yellow snow." Some are limiting, create stress and limit your perspective like, "it doesn't matter what I do," or "everyone I love leaves me."

It was my understanding for a long time that I chose my beliefs and behaviors by carefully evaluating available evidence, using previous experience and intellectual reasoning. Turned out, that happened 5% of the time. Ninety-five percent of the time I was operating from the subconscious (Lipton, 2008).

I can appreciate that some files activated automatically and served me quite well like, "I am good at sports," or "a university degree is beneficial," but I was not aware of many other files that were also operating and were not in my best interest such as;

I need to be taken care of.

Drinking helps me deal with grief.

My success is only worthy if others reward it.

I should not make people upset.

I should not express my emotions.

I should ignore my grief.

Smoking calms my nerves.

Intimate relationships are all about my partner.

I am to be seen, not heard.

People I love leave me.

If I am sick people will take care of me.

I'm bad.

What I DO or achieve is what people love about me.

What others feel, is more important than what I feel.

Don't ask people to do things for me or they'll leave.

Everything happens to me.

It doesn't matter what I do.

Let's take the first one, "I need to be taken care of." No one told me to believe that. I grew up competing with boys and held my own, I lived without a father for most of my life, orphaned at 18 and married for only 14 years. For all accounts and purposes, I was very independent, and it appeared that the evidence supporting the belief, "I need to be taken care of," did not exist. However, the evidence was there and was so extensive; it had a dedicated drawer in the filing cabinet.

In that drawer titled, "I need to be taken care of," it contained files of every experience, every emotion and every thought I ever had as I watched my mother crumble after she lost Dad. Every reaction I had while I observed her sitting there, day after day, sad, overwhelmed and lost got added to the folders in that drawer. The belief, "I need to be taken care of," was supported by mountains of evidence and was emotionally charged. When Mom was taken care of by Dad, everything was great. When Mom was not taken care of by Dad, when he died, she fell apart.

Those limiting beliefs created the foundation by which I would shape the perceptions of my experiences. When encountering a new experience, my mind reached back into my memory searching for other situations that were similar, retrieved the popular action or belief, and responded accordingly. It was a habit. The unconscious mind did this automatically, and I was **not** consciously aware that I was doing that.

If I saw yellow snow, I would reach back into my memory, open the file, connect it to a dog peeing, and react by not eating the snow.

If presented with a loss, I would reach back into my memory, open the file, connect it to other losses, and react the same way. In my case, responding like my mother did when she lost Dad. Stress increased my tendency to revert to old habits (Schwabe and Wolf, 2009).

Even though I was fiercely independent, when life threw me a curve ball it triggered all the emotions, beliefs and experiences in the, "I need to be taken care of" memory drawer, which was connected to the "loss," file and created reactions that were exaggerated and emotionally charged. The curve ball made a connection to dad's death, which made a connection to Mom's reaction and connection to my belief, "I need to be taken care of."

Any situation I experienced as an adult that connected to that drawer and all the files in it triggered the contents. The new situation would become assimilated, and my response to the new situation would be exaggerated or emotionally charged.

Let's try another example. Whenever I got distressed, I would keep my feelings to myself. Being sad, connected to the, "Don't express your emotions" file, which plugged into the "don't make people upset" file, and all the emotions contained in both. My mind reached back linking the files containing the memories of placating Mom, and to the files containing the memories of my partner telling me he would leave me if I got angry. The habitual response in the folder was to avoid expressing my emotions, and that was how I would react to the new situation. In that moment, my calm, easy going attitude and behavior disguised my distress. **That is why limiting beliefs are hard to detect. They mask themselves as positive traits or truths.**

EXAGGERATED RESPONSES

Relationships can be the best breeding ground for limiting beliefs to surface. Significant others or family members are often our best triggers, knowing the exact button to push to get a reaction. I noticed that my hidden hurt or buried grief often surfaced unknowingly, during random, meaningless disagreements surging forth like a broken dam. The exaggerated response frightened me at the time because it was like an ugly cry gone wrong. I didn't know where all the emotion was coming from, and my pattern was to suppress it and I couldn't. Those exaggerated responses continued to reinforce my limiting belief that people could not handle my emotions, and that I needed to bottle them up and bury them deep inside again.

That is what, "you create your experience," means. I behaved in a way that reinforced my limiting thoughts and beliefs, giving them strength and resistance from change. I was keeping the limiting belief alive.

In my relationship, I **unconsciously** married someone who I thought **could take care of me**, made me **feel** whole and interpreted that feeling as love. Just like the way my Dad took care of my Mom. That was my default programming. I married the perfect person that would allow me to play out that limiting belief and other beliefs as well such as,

My feelings don't matter.

People can't handle my emotions.

Lose myself in my marriage.

Don't get angry or upset.

I should not ask for help or people will leave me.

If I get sick, people will love me.

People who love me, leave me.

I'm to be seen and not heard.

And the list goes on. I went into the marriage with a set of beliefs that were unconsciously choosing my behavior and reactions. My partner thought he married a strong, independent woman but what he got was a woman who unconsciously believed that she needed to marry someone to take care of her, that her husband's feelings were more important than hers, and she would do everything she could, not to upset him. It felt like love, but it was not. It was familiarity and comfort disguised as love.

I was at Pizza Delight working one night when the manager's friend came in. When I found out she could give palm readings, I quickly begged her for one. Outstretching my hand, she followed one of the lines in my hand with the tip of her finger and said, "your father died." I was shocked. I could feel the nervous excitement rising inside me. "He died of a blood clot, and the doctors didn't know," she continued, "and if they had, he wouldn't have died." I fell into pieces. All that emotion I had stuffed down inside just exploded to the surface (loss folder). I slowly backed away from her, out the door and drove home, barely able to see through the tears.

I tried to explain to Mom what the palm reader had seen, about how Dad didn't have to die, that the doctors made a mistake and didn't help him fast enough. I desperately wanted her to hear me and comfort me but she fell apart. Right there, she went into hysterics, to a level that matched my hysterics. It was not the response I was looking for. It was not worth explaining why I was upset because she couldn't support me. Folder retrieved? "Don't get angry or upset." Folder response? Shut down.

One day, I got into an argument with my partner just before I was leaving for work. A mere disagreement turned into a full-fledged fight to the point that I did not even know what we were arguing about anymore. I could not get out of it; the argument just kept spiraling and accelerating out of control. Scared I'd be late for work, I left the house, got in my car and started pulling out of the driveway when I saw him punch the glass door. It shattered into a million pieces, cutting his hand, making it bleed and drip down his arm. I kept backing out and headed to work, ignoring his violent response. I didn't know how to calm him down, just as I didn't know how to calm Mom down either. Folder retrieved? "Don't get angry or upset." The unconscious response, shut down.

Over the years, a belief expands and begins to encompass other thoughts and beliefs of similar design. The folders expand and the drawers multiply. For example, the belief, "Don't get angry or upset," included other limiting beliefs as well.

I shouldn't express my emotions.

What I feel does not matter.

Emotions are scary.

Don't make people upset.

It's wrong to feel sad.

Emotions are to be controlled.

I am crazy.

Every time I had the thought, "Don't get angry or upset," I activated the other beliefs; I shouldn't express my emotions; what I feel does not matter; emotions are scary; don't make people upset; it's wrong to feel sad and emotions are to be controlled. One conversation or experience would trigger all those beliefs.

Each belief had strong emotions attached to it too, anchoring it in my unconscious mind so that when it was triggered, the emotions were activated too.

Belief	Emotions Attached
What I feel does not matter	Sad, unhappy, lonely
It's wrong to feel sad	Isolated, shut down, bad
Emotions are scary	Fake, fragile, fatigued, guarded

When I believed, "I shouldn't express my emotions," the feelings of inhibition, sadness, and unhappiness got activated. In addition, the feelings of loneliness, isolation, fatigue, being shut down and guardedness got activated too because my mind had grouped them together. When one belief got activated, the other thoughts and the emotions attached to them became triggered as well, creating an exaggerated response.

CREATING A NEW HABIT OF POSITIVE THINKING

How do we find our limiting beliefs? We find our limiting beliefs by bringing attention and awareness to what we are thinking and feeling. Once we know what we are thinking and feeling, we can examine the thoughts and eliminate the ones that are not serving us.

By questioning my fears and limiting beliefs, increasing my positive thoughts and decreasing my negative thoughts, I was restructuring my unconscious mind. Eventually, a positive reaction became my default even during stressful or challenging circumstances instead of an old habitual negative response from my past. My unconscious started playing a new tape or recording of what I believed to be true bringing more awareness, increased opportunities and maximized my body's ability to heal.

What can you do to increase your positive thoughts and decrease your negative thoughts?

4 STEPS TO INCREASE YOUR POSITIVE THOUGHTS AND DECREASE YOUR NEGATIVE THOUGHTS

1. Identify what you're thinking
2. Question your thoughts
3. Change your thoughts
4. Empower your positive thought with positive emotion

1. Identify what you are thinking

You can't change what you don't acknowledge, so we need to stop your thinking long enough for you to take an inventory of what your thoughts are.

Identifying the thoughts or beliefs that hold up or maintain your fear is a vital step for you to be able to challenge those thoughts, head on. You can talk positively all day long, but if you have a negative, fear-driven, program running unconsciously through your mind all day, the unconscious will take over. The unconscious is more powerful right now because it has momentum. You need to break that momentum, and you do that by interrupting its flow and by challenging its validity.

You are specifically looking for any negative thought or belief. How do you do that? You need to focus your attention on what it is you are thinking. Some strategies you could use to do this include, putting an elastic band around your wrist, a dot on the back of your hand, set your cell phone to go off or whatever else you can come up with to get you to interrupt your activity and focus on your thinking. When you catch your negative thought, write it down, type it out or make note of it somehow before it takes off to thought land again.

Using this strategy, I was able to identify some of the underlying limiting beliefs that operated in the background of my life.

Everyone I love leaves me.

I need to be taken care of.

What's the use?

It doesn't matter what I do.

I don't have enough money.

I'm a burden.

Everything happens to me.

This unconscious program was playing over and over again. I didn't realize it until I started checking in to see what I was thinking.

2. Question your thoughts

Once you have identified a negative thought, question it. Byron Katie (2002), founder of, The Work of Byron Katie, discovered that questioning her thoughts brought her freedom. Her questions were;

Is it true?

Is it true I am going to end up in a wheelchair?

It felt like yes.

Can you absolutely know that it is true?

I'm going to end up in a wheelchair. That moment at age 20 did I absolutely know that I would end up in a wheelchair? No. It was possible, but did I know with absolute certainty that I would? No.

How do you react, what happens, when you believe that thought?

I felt sad, weak, angry, burdened, upset, tired, exhausted, depleted, teary eyed, jealous, unmotivated, disabled, and disempowered.

When you can connect an emotion to a thought or a physiological response to a thought, they all become a neon sign that a limiting belief is active. Eventually, **you won't have to rely only on knowing what you are thinking to be aware a limiting belief is active but will be able**

to tune into a negative feeling or a physical discomfort as additional cues.

Who would you be without the thought?

What difference would it have made, in that moment, emotionally, mentally or physically if I no longer thought that thought?

I would have been present in that moment noticing how my brother and sister took me in, my family and friends supported me, that physically I was no different in that moment.

I highly recommend Byron Katie's book titled, *Loving What Is* to explore further the topic of questioning your stressful thoughts. I attended many of her workshops and the nine-day School for The Work and found her strategy to deal with stressful thoughts was by the far the quickest and most effective way to move beyond them.

Instead of asking, is it true, I began to ask myself **what are the facts**? If I reduce the situation just to the facts without interpreting it, embellishing it, adding blame or judgment I can more easily open myself up to possible solutions or movement forward. For example, I remember a period when tensions were high because my Ex stayed in the house for eight months after he informed me he wanted a divorce and was not leaving until we had a signed separation agreement. Every day he tried to torment me, to break me, to get me to agree to his terms, but I stood my ground reaffirming in my head that the Universe supported me always.

It was his turn to have the kids on our four-day cycle of child custody, and he took them to his girlfriend's house. I usually filled my loneliness with T.V. shows and plopped myself down on the couch after they left. When I clicked the on button, the screen appeared fuzzy, and the satellite programming was not visible. I got up and investigated the wires behind the theater style television and noticed they were all disconnected. My partner had purposely removed them knowing that I didn't understand how to reconnect them with the surround sound, VCR, satellite and T.V., and physically would not be able to hook them up either.

Each action that followed was an example of the baby steps I needed to take to move forward and embrace change. A simple experience would challenge my limiting beliefs, my ability to trust and to be in the moment. The experience was the tool being used to fix my foundation.

I felt instantly a rush of dejection because he had done this to me, but then I **stopped** and isolated the facts. The wires are disconnected. *Everything else I am feeling right now is the story I am telling about it. If I am to watch TV, I will figure out how to reconnect them, if I am not supposed to watch TV I won't and I trust that either is in my best interest. I can do this. I am a strong, powerful, woman capable and intelligent. I can and will do this.* I used my reacher, a thirty-six-inch pole with a handle that grabs things off the floor to help people who can't bend down, to grab the plugs and inserted them where I thought they might go. It was not easy, but calmly I moved them around, hoping for the right combination to bring the picture back on the screen. An hour later, I pressed the on button, and the satellite tuned in. I did it. Despite his attempts to break me, to frustrate me, I did it, and confidence and power surged through my veins.

Also, you can explore your negative thought by asking, "in this moment are you dealing with a real, genuine threat or danger?" Again, another way to get to the facts.

When I projected my dilapidated, lifeless body, sitting in a wheelchair was I dealing with a perceived threat or a real one? It was a perceived threat because, in that moment, I was standing and walking. The fact was, I was given a verbal diagnosis of FSH-MD. That was it. Yesterday I did not have the diagnosis, today I do. That was it. Any stress was a result of what I chose to believe about what it meant to be diagnosed with FSH-MD. The diagnosis was a tool to identify a limiting belief or a crack in my foundation.

3. Change the thought

We have all heard of positive affirmations, which are basically, positive thoughts. We need to create a new habit and like other habits it requires diligence, practice, and more practice to solidify it as a new behavior. To form a habit, a behavior must be carried out repeatedly in the presence of the same contextual cues (Lally et al., 2010). I invite you to change the negative thought to a positive thought and write it down. Some examples of turning a negative thought into a positive thought might include;

NEGATIVE THOUGHT	POSITIVE THOUGHT
I don't have enough money.	My needs are always taken care of.
I am sick	I am healthy, strong and powerful.

I get that this can seem untruthful, as if you are making it up and lying, but this is a necessary starting point to change the negative stream of thoughts you may be having, to positive ones. Think of negative thoughts like water erosion to the foundation of a house. It wears away at the structure, slowly, but powerfully until it creates a crack, and then another crack. Creating a new habit of positive thinking keeps your foundation strong and impenetrable from outside circumstances.

One time, for example, I returned home to find the pathway to the stairs blocked by his car, and bicycles packed in between the wall and his car. I felt my tears forming, not believing he would do this, knowing I physically needed to use the stair lift beyond the obstructions. *Everything is so hard. I don't know if I can take any more of this. I want him to stop bothering me.* I **stopped**. Caught myself thinking negatively. *If I am supposed to get to the door this way, I will be able to clear a path, if not, then I was not supposed to get through.* That connected me, brought presence to the moment. Rather than playing out the story of how he had blocked my way to be mean, I brought presence to the moment by finding the facts. The facts were, the way was blocked. I scanned the carnage and calculated a strategy to see me through it. Feeling it was doable, I proceeded and gained entry. Confidence and power surged.

On another occasion, he was following me, inches from my face, yelling at me, "You're selfish, all you care about is yourself. You don't care about the kids or anything; you are a terrible mother. You only care about money. It is all about you. It's always all about you!" I did not respond but observed my reactions physically, emotionally and mentally. *Leave me alone. Stop hurting me. I don't know how much more I can take. I am breaking. I wish I could run away.* He kept at it, just like John did when I was little trying to break me and getting me to cry. He followed me everywhere; I had no escape, and physically, I was at his mercy since I moved so slowly.

I tried standing in front of the TV with the volume turned high to drown him out and then turned on the blow dryer pretending to do my hair as he berated me over and over again inches from my face. I **stopped** and brought attention to my negative thoughts. I began chanting silently in my head; *I am a powerful being. This is in my best interest; I do not know why this is happening but trust in the Universe. I am strong, capable and powerful beyond measure. I look forward to what the Universe has in store for me. I trust that everything is for me and supports my movement forward. He does not know who he is; He does not feel the loving presence inside him. That is why he acts this way. He is a loving being that is hidden by his limiting beliefs. I am a loving being.* The mantra played over again and again while he spoke. I could hear his voice but stopped listening to what he was saying, hearing only my mantra and feeling the connection and presence of source. I was loving me and trusting the Universe to support me through it, and it did. My partner drifted away, and the challenge passed.

These experiences were the tools being used by the Universe to restructure my foundation. I was the power, the love that surged within me, I was learning to tap into it, to reconnect with it.

4. Empower your positive thought with positive emotion

Grounding a new, positive thought in the unconscious requires the positive thought to have a greater emotional weight than its negative counterpart.

Let's suppose that because you are no longer working, you think you don't have enough money.

Negative thought: I don't have enough money.

Positive thought: I have enough money.

In this moment, you are sitting there, probably in a building, protected from the elements, food easily accessible, water within reach and clothes covering your body.

You don't have enough money. Is that true? What else do you need to buy, right now, in this moment? Do you really require anything else in this moment for your survival?

You have enough money. Does that ring a little truer for you now? You're not pushing a cart with a bag of belongings down an alleyway. You have enough money. Wow? Feel that. Feel the gratitude of knowing you have shelter, a warm bed, food in the fridge and free flowing water at your fingertips. Feel the air as it passes through your nostrils and fills your lungs with life-sustaining oxygen. Feel your heart beating rhythmically, without any effort on your part, giving you life. That gratitude fuels positive emotion behind the thought, "I have enough money."

Can you own the thought, "I have enough money?" Is it believable now? Does it have a positive emotional charge?

Negative thought: *It's not fair. I hate this disease.*

Stop. Flip it. Make it positive.

Positive thought: *Muscular Dystrophy is a gift.*

I needed to find examples to support it. How is MD a gift? I started writing and below, is what came to me. At first, it can be difficult but try to find an example. Once you find one, find another one.

- I get to stay home with my kids
- Have time to do scrapbooking
- Explored spirituality
- Get close parking spots
- I get a discount on taxes
- I get preferred seating
- I don't have to stand in line at amusement parks
- It requires me to go deeper into myself
- My children get academic help from me and are A students
- I cook healthier foods
- I can attend my children's assemblies and school activities
- I save money on housecleaning
- I don't need to buy work clothes
- Save on gas because I don't have to drive to work
- I get to hang out with women in my neighborhood who are, stay at home moms
- I avoid crowds because I shop during the daytime during the work week
- I swim in my pool on work days
- I experience how my body adapts
- I learned to face my fears
- I learned not rely on my outer appearance
- I learned not to rely on my physical strength
- I learned to surrender

- I learned to love myself
- I learned to slow down
- I notice little things like the crack in pavement, curbs, wind, temperature
- I meet people I would not have otherwise met
- I learned that walkers are great for carrying your bags
- I get discount movie tickets
- I board the plane first
- I learned to meditate
- I learned that planning is not necessarily safer
- I learned that being safe...doesn't always feel good
- I don't have to wear high heels
- I don't have to wait at customs at the airport
- No one expects me to help them move

I had to repeat this exercise many times because the negative charge of *I hate muscular dystrophy*, was formidable. I needed to create a charge stronger than that one, to help anchor the thought, "muscular dystrophy is a gift," in my unconscious mind, and form the new habit.

Changing an old habit and creating a new habit takes time. Researchers have found that it takes between 18 to 254 days to create a new habit (Lally et al. 2010) because your old habits automatically activate based on environmental cues (Walker et al. 2014). Don't despair. They are just thoughts. By practicing the four steps above, you'll train your mind to automatically retrieve a positive thought instead of a negative one, keeping you connected and open to infinite possibilities.

MIRRORING

Mirroring is a way in which the Universe shows us our belief patterns by reflecting back to us what needs to be worked on, identifiable by our reaction.

1. That which we hate in others is what we deny most within ourselves.
2. That which we deny within us, we believe to be true.

If you had said to me, "you like being dependent on someone," I would have denied it until I was red in the face and given you 50 examples of how that was ludicrous. I would have spewed off hundreds of instances where I acted independently and told you how crazy you were. "How dare you say that to me?" That negative emotionally charged reaction would be a telltale sign that it was a limiting belief. Somewhere, I believed that I needed to be taken care of.

Any adverse reaction, stressful thought, annoyance, etc. is your neon sign or tool, telling you that a limiting belief is active within you. Unconsciously, a file gets triggered, firing off the programmed emotional response showing up in the moment as stress, annoyance, judgment, etc.

I struggled with this one. It meant that everything I criticized, judged, compared or saw as wrong in others was pointing to the very thing I unconsciously believed to be true about myself. If you are serious about finding happiness independent of outside circumstances, acknowledging that these beliefs exist, is imperative.

I believed myself to be a shining example of someone who was cool, calm and collected because I rarely showed my emotions. That's why when Brenda, the intuitive, told me that I was angry I thought, *"if you're looking for anger, then you should talk to my partner. He's the one with all the anger. It's like you're saying it's all my fault, I can't help it that all these things have happened to me."* To say that I was angry seemed bizarre to me but because of my denial and trying to attribute it to someone else, it was my neon sign or the tool being used to tell me that I **was**, in fact angry.

I needed to find where that belief was true within me.

But I couldn't find it and didn't believe it. *Where's the anger? Am I angry at Mom? Am I angry at Dad? Am I angry at my partner? Am I angry at God? I don't feel it. I don't feel my face getting red, and I am not clenching my fists or stomping my feet.* I couldn't connect to it.

I knew there had to be anger within me because of my negative reaction to it. I needed to find a way to tap into it. So, I took a bat and started hitting my pillow on my bed with the intention of finding the anger and yelled out with each hit, whatever came to mind. At first, it felt awkward, foreign and uncomfortable, but I kept at it until something came to me.

"I hate being sick. I hate not being able to do what I want. I hate that my Mom and Dad died. I hate that I feel alone. I hate that I hurt. I hate that my partner had an affair. I hate feeling sad all the time." I started hitting harder and yelling louder. "I hate being in a state of chaos. I hate God. I hate that it doesn't matter what I do because something bad always happens to me." I made a connection. I could feel the tears forming and my insides loosened as I released more and more with each hit. "I hate that no one really loves me. I'm fucking tired!" My body began to feel lighter, and the sensation of sleepiness came over me. All the energy that was being used to hold in and deny the anger seemed to be released and suddenly available.

Allowing and freely feeling and expressing myself invited that part of myself (anger), to surface and release. I no longer had the need to hold it in, bury or suppress it because I was inviting it to be part of me rather than denying that it existed.

My blood would boil when people suggested to me that I was sick because I wanted the attention. How dare people insinuate that I wanted to be in pain, that I wanted to be living this hell? But truth existed in my angered response and deep down I felt that perhaps they were right.

My mother's demonstrations of affection were rare, but as a child I felt her love through the cold washcloth she folded and placed gently on my feverish forehead when I was sick. She never told me she loved me, but when she came to me and performed this small gesture, comfort, security and warmth would wash over me. I ached to feel that as an adult, and I believe I created a reality for myself to get it. My unconscious mind was trying to get relief; to feel the way I did when my mother came to me.

Acknowledging the belief and my part in creating my experience allowed me to own it. For it to become a part of me. Moving forward, I could consciously choose more effective ways to find comfort, security, and warmth, therefore, creating a new folder of positive beliefs and emotions in my unconscious.

In my coaching practice, I find that clients actively resist the concept of mirroring. One of them said, "a person butted in line, and I was furious. He was so rude!" When I invited my client to explore that part of himself, he assured me that he was not rude. However, his negative, agitated response was a clear indicator that he was, in fact, rude and was resisting that part of himself. His reaction was notifying him about a crack in his foundation and that experience in line was an opportunity to patch it up. By identifying an example in his life where he may have been rude, he could begin to absorb that quality of rudeness into his Being. Eventually, a person will butt in front of him or cut him off in traffic in the future, and there will be no reaction within him. He will have patched the crack.

If you find yourself reacting to or denying a personal quality, I would encourage you to get quiet and invite that quality in. When in your life have you been that? Just one time. If you open yourself up to it, an example will appear, and your emotional, mental and physical body will start to relax a bit. If you can, try to find another. Every quality you deny creates resistance and takes up your valuable energy to keep it suppressed. Letting go of the resistance frees up your energy and opens you up to more possibilities.

PEELING BACK THE ONION

Limiting beliefs have multiple layers like an onion and the biggest onion, I had was the, "I need someone to take care of me," onion.

It showed up in my marriage and when I faced new challenges. I peeled away layer after layer until one day, it just fell away. I hired a lawyer, Peter Pooglas, to take over my family court case. I hated to think about wasting money but it felt necessary. There was some relief in knowing he'd take care of the paperwork, that I could rely on his knowledge of court protocol and his familiarity with the system.

Contacting his office, I was surprised to hear he was on his honeymoon and would not be returning for two weeks before the settlement conference. The timing made me uneasy.

I asked his assistant, "Will he have enough time to prepare?"

"Yes, no problem," she assured me.

Peter's office served the court brief, financial statement, and Form 14C in preparation for the settlement conference days away.

I quickly checked my emails and noticed an attachment from Peter's assistant. Skimming the formal introductions to the first paragraph, I felt panic rising as I read, "This is to advise that Peter Pooglas was appointed to be a judge; as a consequence, he can no longer act for you in your legal matter."

My court date was five days away, and I didn't have a lawyer. I had worked for just under two years on this, on my own and now when I needed someone more than ever, they dropped my case. He was supposed to take care of me. I felt sick to my stomach as I mentally scanned my options.

I thought, *"I know this is in my best interest, it has to be. I am totally supported. This is absolutely for me. The solution is there. Step back, the solution has to be there."* I knew this to be true, but my body believed otherwise, as heat moved through my veins and my face flushed with fear.

This is absolutely in my best interest. This needs to happen this way. Everything is for me. I hear my words, but it doesn't stop the thought of going into the courtroom and having the opposing counsel or the judge berating me, or the dreadful image of a young, ill-prepared, uninterested replacement lawyer forced to represent me at the last minute.

I know the solution is there. I may not see it right now, but it's there, I reaffirm to myself. But...then....I feel it. Here

I go again. First, I start to feel like a victim; everything always happens to me. Second, the tears come, and this nauseating fear-based panic and sense of wanting to give up overwhelms any possible influence of positive affirmations. Sitting back in my chair, I observe my reaction, the tears, the aloneness, the barrage of images of all the things that are now going to happen projected far into the future, homeless, disabled, impoverished. I know that it won't happen, but I can't stop it. It's out of context. My reaction is so over exaggerated. It's crazy. I know it's crazy. I recognize it. I allow it. I feel it. Acknowledge it and observe. Then I make a plan.

That's enough. I can do this. I wish I knew someone who would know what to do. I need help. I need to call someone. Who can I call? My mind is so busy with its chatter and negative projections that I know it's closing myself off from possible solutions. I pick up the phone and call Kath, my friend from University and then I call Patty, who I have known since grade seven. They help me develop a plan, and my anxiety starts to dissipate.

The phone rings and I answer in anticipation, "Hello."

"Hello, is this Lori? It's Ms. McInniston," the replacement lawyer.

"Both of the remaining lawyers here have six years of experience, but it is well within your right to seek council outside this office."

"I understand I have that option, but you can imagine my concern regarding the short time frame. If you were me Ms. McInniston, whom would you recommend either in your firm or outside?"

She agreed to help me get the case adjourned due to Mr. Pooglas's appointment and Ms. McInniston supports and arranges for me to meet a new lawyer before the new settlement conference.

A month later, on our court date while lying in bed I set my intention for a peaceful, fair resolution.

The intensity of the judicial system was hard to miss as I entered the doors. Placing my side bag that usually hangs from my right-hand wheelchair arm into the plastic tray, along with my keys and water bottle, I waited in line to enter the metal detector.

"Drive through here please and spread out your arms," the officer moved the scanner under my arms and over my body leaving a two-inch barrier of air in between.

"Go on through," the officer said, and I pulled out my belongings from the tray that had just passed through the scanner, doing my best not to hold up the line.

Fixed steel chairs, back to back, sit between the courtroom entrances and private consulting offices along the far wall. I find a space at the end of the row. I can recall everything now, as if it were yesterday.

Ms. Biller, my attorney, arrives, wearing a conservative gray skirt and matching blazer with a slightly darker trim on the collar and directs me over to a quiet space so that we can talk privately. "I just wanted to ask you a few things," she said. We sit facing each other but, she is a bit distracted as her eyes focused on something just over my left shoulder. I stay where I am, my attention directly on her, well aware of the time crunch before we see the judge.

She says, "It's your husband, he is really upset. His lawyer is no longer with the firm, and his previous lawyer is on vacation, so they have sent him a new one. I don't think he knew about it. I wasn't told directly but heard through the grapevine; his attorney left the firm. He doesn't look happy."

Still looking at Ms. Biller, I don't turn around. I know what she is watching; I have seen it a thousand times. His face is probably getting red, and he is stomping around taking deep breaths and letting the air come out his mouth making a "Huff," sound. He's mad and frustrated.

"He is turning really red, I think he is about to explode," she reports still looking over my left shoulder. I still don't turn. There is no enjoyment in watching him deconstruct again and again. My lawyer is trying to bring her eyes and thoughts back to my case, but I see her curiosity getting the better of her as she struggles to bring her attention back to the papers in front of her. I wait, watching her as her eyes grow larger, taking in the spectacle behind me. As though convincing herself to look away she says, "O.K.....," and turns her body to sit directly in front of me and grabs her papers with both hands. My partner is reacting to his limiting beliefs, just as I had days before.

"Let me talk to his attorney, to get a handle on their position." Ms. Biller heads toward the glass doors. I venture over near Courtroom five's doors and sit with my iPad, checking emails when I catch a glimpse of my partner heading toward me. It is awkward as I looked up and softly said, "Hi."

With a tense face and slight sneer, he looked me straight in the eye and said, "You're evil."

I feel nothing. No agitation, no upset, no shock. I have no reaction. It feels good not to be triggered. I know this is done. I can love him. Not in a, "I love you, want to jump your bones," kind of love, but can see him as a loving being, who is believing his limiting thoughts.

Turning my attention back to my iPad, I continue to look through my emails.

Ms. Biller opens the interior glass door and walks through, folders stacked and held in place by the crux of her arm and a rolling square black case, pulled by the other arm. "Let's find a place to talk." Ms. Biller searched for an empty consultation room, entered, holding open the door for me to wheel inside.

"Well, I thought we should discuss his position about the three core issues. I don't believe we are too far off but they believe there should be no back child support." She points to a chart, outlined on the paper in front of us, explaining their reasoning and calculations which I disagree with.

"It just is not right that he can kick his daughter out, quit his job, cancel their health insurance......." I stop. "But....it doesn't matter that it's not right does it?"

"No, it doesn't. Let me talk to them and have them show us their calculations and we will go from there."

I am not happy with the idea of having to settle for less than what I deserve, but I also knew deep down that the details didn't matter. Calm and connected, I felt like the case would get resolved that day. The change in lawyers created the dynamics for it to happen. It was as if the Universe rose, held my hand and led me through, minute by minute, with no effort on my part. I was being cared for, cradled, and I was open to it, seeing the support as universal.

The lawyers went back and forth for the rest of the day until they gave me a hand drafted version of the agreement.

"Just need you to initial each page, the changes and then sign and date it on the last page," said Ms. Biller.

It was ridiculous really, seeing the handwritten scribble of compromise on two pages, representing two years, of two people, trying to control their projected outcome when in the end, it just sort of happened as if it was always supposed to end that way. The terrorizing thought projected future I had imagined over and over again if the legal decision had been anything other than the one I wanted again, as always, never materialized.

The only thing left to do was bring the case before the judge. Ms. Biller and I moved out into the common area outside courtroom five and waited for an opportunity to finalize everything. As we chatted about our children, my partner hovered, making loops around the waiting area, walking briskly, around and around and around.

I imagine that his thoughts were terrorizing him. Perhaps he was projecting a destitute future, a vision of a miserable world, crippling his spirit and limiting his possibilities or maybe not. I don't judge him in that moment because I know how easily my thought-provoked perspective can change my world and what he was experiencing was none of my business. What was my business, was me, and right then, in that moment I was able to feel the peace, flow in, out and around the body like the fresh air of an open window and I was grateful.

The layers of the onion peel back as you bring awareness to your emotions and the thinking behind them. Eventually, the belief loses its charge as you develop more and more evidence that the belief is not true for you.

PRACTICE AND REFLECTION

The Practice and Reflection section at the end of each chapter is your opportunity to explore what might be keeping you from finding happiness regardless of circumstances. Taking action is critical to you moving forward in your life and the exercises provided were created to help you do that.

1. Identify your negative thoughts and record them in the chart below. Practice changing your negative thoughts to positive thoughts and infuse them with new, positive emotion.

Negative thought	Question your negative thought. Is it true? What are the facts? Real or imagined?	Turn the negative thought into a positive thought	Infuse the positive thought with positive emotion
I need more money.	No. In this moment, I don't need any more money.	I have enough money.	I am not hungry. I have shelter. I have water, food, clothes, friends, family, I am warm.

2. When you check in to see what you are thinking, observe and record the feelings associated with it. Are you mad, sad, frustrated? Does your stomach turn or does your skin feel hot?

Negative thought	Emotions	Physical Reactions	Other connected thoughts
I can't take this anymore.	Sad, low, isolated, lonely, scared, vulnerable	Weak, fragile, upset stomach, tired, exhausted	I've got nothing left. Why is this happening to me? Everything happens to me. It doesn't matter what I do.

3. Mirroring. Record any negative thoughts or statements you make about other people, invite it in with an "I am" statement and find an example in your life where you ARE that. This is about inviting in what you are denying or resisting within yourself. Invite it in, and then let it go.

Negative thought or statement	I am........	Example
That guy is rude for cutting me off.	I am rude for cutting people off. I am rude. I cut people off.	I have cut someone off while driving. I have cut people off in conversations. I have cut myself off from being friends with some people. I am rude when I don't listen.

4. Making the connection. Review your responses in exercises 1-3 and ask yourself the following questions.

  A. Are there any negative **beliefs** that are similar?

  B. Are there negative **emotions** that are similar?

  C. Does your response seem exaggerated or over-charged? If yes, when have you felt this way before? What is your earliest memory of that response or feeling?

5. Take that earlier memory and complete the chart below.

Negative thought	Question your negative thought. Is it true? What are the facts? Real or imagined?	Turn the negative thought into a positive thought	Infuse the positive thought with positive emotion
I need more money.	No. In this moment, I don't need any more money.	I have enough money.	I am not hungry. I have shelter. I have water, food, clothes, friends, family, I am warm.
I didn't have enough money for bread and milk at the grocery store after mom died	No. Someone gave me the money at the checkout.	I had enough money.	The Universe provided the money. I had the perfect amount of money.

CHAPTER FOUR: FEAR

Fearful and negative thinking can be invisible. It can happen all day long without our being aware of it, but the effects can be quite powerful. It's kind of like a food processor. When you overload it by putting a whole bunch of stuff in it, it just explodes, and you're left cleaning up the mess. It would be much easier to take the time to put less food in for a couple of extra batches, than the time it would take to clean up the mess afterward.

The same is true for negative thinking. It is much easier to take the time to clean up your negative, fearful thoughts now, before they create a mess of problems later on, physiologically, mentally, emotionally and behaviorally.

Fear can also be a gift. It lets you know that you are no longer connected or enjoying your journey. It can bring your attention to an outdated, limiting belief and give you the opportunity to change it.

Is your thinking processor overfilled with fearful or negative thoughts?

THE POWER OF FEARFUL THINKING

☛ Do you have **terrifying thoughts** of what the future holds and spending your days worrying about it?

I remember imagining myself bedridden and completely dependent. I imagined myself unable to have children or not be able to care for them. I imagined being alone. I imagined falling and not being able to get up. The fear just got bigger and bigger and more debilitating as time went on. But you know what? None of it happened, it was a complete waste of energy.

☛ Is your thinking **incessant**?

Are you continually rehearsing over and over again, what has happened, is happening or shouldn't have happened to you? Does that type of thinking preoccupy your everyday life?

My thoughts were relentless, and I needed a way to stop them. I consistently projected what would happen if I didn't have enough money, if he did this or if my partner did that, and devised plans in my head about how to deal with them. I couldn't seem to stop because every time I brought awareness to what I was thinking, I found I was regurgitating the same train of thought over and over again, especially when it came to my health. What if I need a wheelchair, what if I can't take care of myself, what if I fall? I am in so much pain. I wish it would stop. I am so tired. I wish I had the energy I had before. I feel terrible. I am feeling really sick. My stomach hurts, etc.

☛ Do you focus on the **worst case scenario**?

Are you claiming the worst-case scenario as your <u>only</u> possible outcome and thinking your life is over?

Like Brenda said, "I had no pictures." I saw nothing in my future and was waiting to die. I saw no other outcome.

☛ Are your thoughts **looping**?

Do you go over and over all the possible negative things that may or may not happen? Do the thoughts loop, repeating over and over again and you're unable to turn them off?

At one time my children joined a Toronto talent agency, requiring me to drive them into the city an hour away for auditions and appointments. Every location was different, and I never knew if there would be stairs or obstacles that I would not be able to maneuver. I planned for hours and hours in my head all the problems that could arise and came up with possible solutions. I would go over them again and again without realizing it, believing that the process was making me feel better, but instead, it was increasing my anxiety. I was stressing before I went, the whole way there and the whole way back.

One day I realized, that not once did I ever encounter an obstacle that could not be dealt with easily. All the fear, planning and stress was all in my head and a complete waste of energy.

☛ Are you waking up in the middle of the night and find your thoughts just **picking up where they left off** the night before, looping again, again?

Out of complete exhaustion, I would finally fall asleep only to awaken a few hours later, thinking again, right from where I left off. It never stopped. The thoughts kept coming and never let me go.

THE IMPACT OF FEAR ON THE BODY

What I learned was that the worrying, projecting and the fear was not helping me but hurting me. The worrying was detrimental to my ability to heal.

How does our body react to fear? Instinctually, our body has a fight or flight mechanism built in to sustain our survival. When we experience the fear of falling, for example, our body reacts by physiologically responding in a way that maximizes its ability to survive the perceived danger.

Heart beats faster

Muscles contract

Breathing becomes rapid

Increases blood sugar

Increases blood pressure

Suppresses the immune system (Flight or Fight Response, Wikipedia)

We would react the same way if a lion were chasing us. Our fight or flight reaction kicks in, maximizing our ability to escape the present perceived danger.

What is so fascinating though is that when we have a fearful thought, let's say about our future or our health, our fight or flight mechanism can kick in the same way it would if lions chased us.

When a fearful thought creates an emotionally charged reaction to fear, sadness, or anger, that emotional reaction becomes a trigger for the fight or flight response to engage. Even though the thought is just a thought and not a present moment or true threat, the body reacts the same way. The emotional response to negative thoughts, conscious or unconscious, makes the body believe it is in real danger, even though it is not. "To the body, a worrisome, fearful thought means, I am in danger, and it responds accordingly, ... The heart beats faster, muscles contract, breathing becomes rapid (Tolle, 2005, p. 134)."

Placebo and the Nocebo effect examples can demonstrate how our body responds to our thinking.

The Placebo effect is observed when a fake treatment or an inactive substance like sugar, distilled water, or saline solution – can sometimes improve a patient's condition simply because the person has the expectation or the belief that it will be helpful.

The Nocebo effect, on the other hand, is a fake treatment or an inactive substance like sugar, distilled water, or saline solution -- can sometimes worsen a patient's condition simply because the person has a negative expectation that they can cause harm.

In a clinical drug trial, (Ted Kaptchuk et al., 2006), an associate professor at Harvard Medical School, found that his patients were experiencing negative and positive side effects of the treatments offered. Half were receiving pain killers, and the other half were getting acupuncture treatments.

What was fascinating about the side effects was that both treatments were placebos. The pills were made of cornstarch, and the acupuncture needles were retractable and never pierced the skin.

"Researchers have found that placebo treatments--interventions with no active drug ingredients--can stimulate real physiological responses, from changes in heart rate and blood pressure to chemical activity in the brain, in cases involving pain, depression, anxiety, fatigue, and even some symptoms of Parkinson's (Feinberg, 2013)."

A thought or an experience perceived as negative can trigger an adverse physiological response because that judgment of that thought or experience being negative is attached to fear. The body is automatically responding to our thinking.

If you are experiencing a health challenge, you often try to do everything in your power to heal by seeing doctors, engaging in therapy, taking medications, eating well and yet, on the other hand, your thinking may be negating your efforts by stressing out your body. By actively engaging in incessant, catastrophic, negative, fearful thinking, your body would be reacting as if, lions were always chasing it. It would be constantly in a flight or fight reaction drawing valuable energy and resources away from the very organs that may be required to maximize your body's ability to heal.

Negative Thoughts can create stress. Experiencing a physical limitation, a loss or being faced with a challenge can lead to incessant thinking about your future. The not knowing of what your future holds, can lead your mind to prophesize, usually in a what if, worse case scenario.

What if I can't work?

What if I can't pay my bills?

What if I can't golf?

What if I can't take care of myself?

What if...

And with each what if, the mind visualizes a perceived future, creating an imagined experience that feels, and looks real. This imaginary experience is so real to us that it creates a reaction, physiologically, emotionally, mentally and behaviorally as though it was happening, right then and there.

We imagine the "what if," worse case scenario, and the realness of it tricks the body into thinking it is happening, and it responds accordingly. These repetitive, powerful thoughts keep us in a perpetual state of stress.

Stress can affect your body, your thoughts, feelings, and your behavior (Mayo Clinic Staff, 2013).

Physiological effects of stress

Headache

Muscle tension or pain

Chest pain

Fatigue

Change in sex drive

Stomach upset

Sleep problems

Emotional effects of stress

Anxiety

Restlessness

Lack of motivation or focus

Irritability

Anger

Sadness or depression

Mental effects of stress

Lack of focus and concentration

Behaviors associated with long-term stress
Overeating or under eating
Angry outbursts
Drug or alcohol abuse
Tobacco use
Social withdrawal

Stress can also contribute to health problems, such as high blood pressure, heart disease, obesity, and diabetes.

When first diagnosed, I believed the worst possible thing that could happen would be to end up in a wheelchair. Where did that thought come from? I had never been in a wheelchair. I didn't know anyone with FSH Muscular Dystrophy. I didn't even know anyone who used a wheelchair. I was convinced, wholeheartedly that I would indeed spend the rest of my life utterly useless and lifeless. I spent weeks crying and sobbing. The fearful thought of my limited future haunted me.

Not much changed physically for ten years until after that second stroke when I heard the doctor say, "the MD has progressed and is affecting your legs." Again, I was enveloped with the vision of me slouched in a wheelchair, lifeless, a burden to my family. I thought my life was over.

Where did those images originate? I had never been in a wheelchair. I didn't know anyone in a wheelchair, and I had not seen anyone with FSH Muscular Dystrophy. I believed my future was undeniably determined, with no exceptions. It was over. The fearful thought of my limited future haunted me.

Sixteen years after that, I was still walking but with the help of a walker. I was walking, but my next step consumed my every thought. I had to ensure my foot was secure and my body was aligned and balanced. I carefully scanned the ground for obstructions, a rock, a crack or curb cut. My mind registered the weather and its impact. Was it windy, slippery, wet? I was walking, but at a price.

One day, I was returning home, walking down the hallway to my condo, when it happened. My foot caught the carpet, and my upper body fell forward. Still standing but bent awkwardly over the walker, I gripped the handles tightly, contemplating my options. Do I fall, to the floor? Do I call for help? I was stuck. I couldn't straighten up, and I was afraid to go to the ground for fear I wouldn't be able to reach the door handle. *Shit! What the hell am I going to do now?*

Somehow, I inched slowly to my neighbor's door, still bent over the walker and managed to bang my head on his door. *Oh God. I can't believe this is happening to me.* The dog barked, but no one came. *Oh shit, they probably can't see me through the peephole. Really? Is this really happening right now?* Still bent over and out of view, I banged my head again. I felt embarrassed when he answered the door, "Ummm, can you help me straighten up?" Without hesitation, he grabbed my shoulders and helped me to stand upright.

The important thing was that I was still walking, right?

Where did that thought come from, that walking is to be preferred? That a person was more whole, healthy and could only have a full life...as long as they were walking?

I made a decision that day. I set out to buy a wheelchair. When I did, my whole world opened up. I had every minute of every day available to me to just BE. I listened to the birds, I felt the wind on my skin and splashed through slush. I got groceries, browsed through department stores and got toilet paper at Costco. All within two hours. I started swimming at the local pool since I was no longer worried about slipping and fatigue. I toured the waterfront on sunny days and watched movies at the theater. I concentrated on what people were saying rather than focusing on my every step.

As it turned out, the worst possible thing that could happen was NOT ending up in a wheelchair, but having the negative thoughts about it. The worst possible thing was creating a negative, frightening image of an experience that in twenty-eight years never happened. The energy, missed opportunities, and sadness could have been avoided if I had merely questioned my thoughts along the way. The end game was the same but the journey to get there, could have been entirely different. Twenty-eight years of thoughts about worry and fear of being in a wheelchair did nothing but create twenty-eight years of worry and fear about being in a wheelchair. It was a choice to believe those thoughts.

Was I right to worry about the disease progression and the need for a wheelchair? Sure. It was my life, and it was my choice to believe whatever I wanted. I was doing my best, with what I knew at the time. Looking back, though...would I do things differently? Probably. Here's why. I know better. When you know better...you can do better.

What I can recognize now is that it did not matter if the threat was real or perceived as real. The effect of believing that my life would be over because I'd end up in a wheelchair caused an automatic physiological, negative, reaction within me. That included rapid breathing, increased blood pressure and blood sugar, a suppressed immune system and emotional and mental stress. For 28 years, I was not dealing with a real threat or danger, but my body sure thought I was.

I had a coaching client that had a goal to complete her high school diploma. As soon as she got close to completing her last course she would sabotage her efforts by finding other things to spend her time on. I could see that she was frightened and stressed by the idea of completing her goal. Upon further investigation, I found that she linked her reaction to an earlier time in her childhood when she had felt the same way. As a child, her father used to invent things in the basement and the whole family celebrated their father's efforts. She felt excitement while he worked on the project but would become fearful as he approached completion. The client shared that every time her father completed a project, he would immediately destroy it in a fit of rage. Without realizing it, she had taken on the belief (created a file in her mind) that it feels good to create something but feels bad to complete it. As an adult, every time she had an idea she would put all her energy and resources into it, but when it came near fruition, she sabotaged it.

Stress and fear were the tools we used to identify that a limiting belief was active within her. Once we identified the limiting belief we devised a plan to walk through the fear, created positive affirmations that were true for her (new folder) and infused them with positive emotion to counterbalance the charge of the limiting belief. After achieving her high school diploma, that experience got added to the new folder and the feeling of accomplishment positively charged it. By creating a plan and walking through fear, she was also adding to her toolbox because she had strategies she could utilize in similar situations in the future.

PRACTICE AND REFLECTION

1. A mantra is a phrase that you can repeat to yourself to empower you in the moment. Read the mantra below or create an empowering mantra for yourself that you can repeat out loud or in your head during fearful times.

I am NOT this experience. This experience is NOT who I am. I am more than an experience or my reaction to it. I am an incredibly powerful Being. This experience is FOR me. It is a tool being used to draw me inward and closer to the essence of who I am. This experience is letting me know that I am reacting to fear because of the thoughts I am believing. I am more than this experience, more than my fears, and I am more than my thoughts.

I may not know why this is happening but trust that it is drawing me closer to who I really am. I may be developing critical skills that I will need to draw on. I might be working through the barriers that have kept me from achieving my goals. This experience is necessary, important and vital to my growth. I know this because it is happening. Everything is for me. Everything is a gift if I choose to look for it. In this moment, I choose to see the gifts.

I am an incredibly powerful being having an extremely impressive experience. I am amazing just because I was born. Nothing is required of me to be amazing. I choose to own my amazingness! The world awaits the gifts that only I can share. I choose to do what it takes today to reconnect with who I really am.

2. What imagined, fearful thoughts of the future keep you from being in the moment?

Fearful Thought.	Real or Imagined?	Emotions or physiological response.	Connections to other negative thoughts.	Earliest memory of similar fearful or connected thought.	Turn it into a Positive thought.	Infuse positive thought with positive emotion. Find examples of how the positive thought is true.

∾☉℘

CHAPTER FIVE: WHO AM I?

An illness, job loss, or a change in a relationship can create a loss of identity that is intensified because of role changes. These role changes may be unseen barriers to you finding happiness because they are attached to external stimuli that have changed.

5 AREAS WHERE YOU CAN EXPERIENCE ROLE CHANGES

1. Work
2. Friends
3. Family
4. Leisure/Community
5. Church/Spiritual

1. Work

You often get more from a job than just a paycheck. You have relationships with your associates, colleagues, and supervisors, accomplish daily goals, have responsibilities, gain recognition, social connections and experience a sense of belongingness. A yearning and a desire for things to go back to the way they were can arise when you can no longer work.

Your job becomes part of your identity when you see yourself AS that job or profession. When this happens, it develops into a role that you play, impacting you and those around you. Next time you are at a social event, watch how you or others treat professionals or react in their presence. You might find in the company of a doctor, for example, people are more respectful, attentive, careful of their comments, engaged and even stand straighter. If you're a doctor used to this reception, it can be difficult to spend each day void of those experiences. This is not about judging people; this is about observing and making note of how we generalize and attribute personality characteristics to people in certain professions. By doing so, you can then reflect on your perspectives and their impact on your life.

Go to a party and within minutes someone will ask you, "so what do you do?" What do you say if you're sick, on long-term disability or can't work anymore? You might want to say, librarian, for example, but because you're not actively working, it doesn't feel true, almost as though you are lying. Responding with, "I used to....," or "I'm on disability right now...," does not seem to fit either and can feel awkward as the words roll off your tongue and out of your mouth. Replies can be challenging because if you say, "I'm on disability," you spend the evening talking about your illness, and if you say nothing, people end up ignoring you.

If you are a highly regarded professional who finds him or herself at home dealing with a health challenge, you may very well be experiencing life through a different role than you are used to. You may no longer be the go-to person; someone else may have had to take over your responsibilities and your connection with others in your work environment may have declined. You might experience people treating you like a "sick," person, rather than the confident, skillful professional you are.

I found myself sitting on the couch, fatigued, in pain, depressed and thinking, *I don't know who I am anymore.* I was not who I used to be. I was not working, socializing, contributing, exciting or growing. I wanted desperately to get my old life back, and when I thought about all that I was NOT, it hurt, and it made things worse. I had lost my identity. Who was I if I was not a teacher?

2. Friends

You play a role as a friend and friends play a role for you, each assigned with particular characteristics and behaviors. During a health crisis, your expectations of friends and family may change by wanting them to be more compassionate, nurturing, sympathetic, or loving and when they can't meet those expectations, you blame them for not being the person you want them to be. However, their original role is who they are and who they have always been. They are not doing anything differently than they have always done. They are showing up as themselves, playing the same role they have always played. You wanting them to be different or play a different role is like asking a bear to be a cat or a tree to be a rock. The more you want them to be who they are not, the more stressed you'll become, because chances are if they were not nurturing before, they won't be nurturing now and wanting them to be something they are not is like wanting a tree to be a rock.

Being a friend to others is also a role, a unique niche that only you can fill. You show up in the lives of others as their friend with particular characteristics that they count on and expect. It could be that you're the one they lean on, look to for comic relief, financial advice, professional wisdom, and so on. During a challenge, when they look to you to fill that role the same way you have always done, and you can't be that for them, they might back away. They are looking for you to be the same, to fulfill the original role that you played.

This is not about judgment or questioning whether or not you or someone else is a good or a bad friend. It is about breaking down the causes of your stress surrounding an illness or challenge and considering that your frustration and sadness may be, partly due to role changes or rigid expectations of how you and others should be.

Being aware that this is occurring allows you to gain a new perspective and open yourself up to different responses. Instead of using your valuable energy to concentrate on what shouldn't be happening, what others should be doing or should have done, you can reclaim it. Bring it back in for your healing. Imagine being a silent witness to your transformation. Yes, transformation. This experience is an invitation to go inward, to have that relationship and be that friend you so desperately want, to yourself.

The potential emptiness you find in old friendships may be that your challenge has transformed you, requiring you to go within and rediscover who you really are.

3. Family

You may be a sibling, a child, a mother, father, or a grandparent and as a result, fill a role or many roles within the family unit. Just like your friends, the people in your family look to you to fill a role and you, look to them to fill a role. When an illness or disability, a death, or job loss, for example, surfaces within the unit, those expectations change, causing a change in the relationship. Society, cultures, and families collectively contribute to the role dynamic, determining the expectations of each. What characteristics does your role entail? Protector, caregiver, breadwinner, supporter, nurturer, fixer, etc.? When you can no longer fill your role based on the expectations of yourself or others, it can be devastating. In the present moment, you may not only be dealing with your challenge. You may also be dealing with the limiting beliefs of the past, projected fears of the future and influences from role changes.

I had an expectation of myself that I would work full time until I was old enough to retire, and had never considered staying at home. When my health prevented me from working, I tried to step into the idea of what I thought a stay at home Mom would be and created expectations for myself in this new role. I continually tried to do what I used to be able to do or what I wanted to do but because of the physical limitations and fatigue issues, I often overextended myself to the point of pain and exhaustion. When we decided to send the kids to daycare to reduce my physical stress, fatigue, and exhaustion, I became even more depressed. Not only was I no longer able to work outside the home, but I was also incapable of being a stay-at-home mom too.

Everyone kept telling me just to relax, take it easy; it was OK for me not do so much. But in my mind, if I didn't do everything I thought I should be doing, I was failing or not contributing enough. A vicious cycle of setting unrealistic expectations for myself and trying to complete them to the point of physical pain ensued. It was not that I wanted to be sick or hurting, but I was attempting to do what I had always done to get what I had always got. I wanted to feel valued, loved, to be needed and appreciated and the only way I knew how to feel that was by <u>doing</u> something. I had a strong, unconscious belief that I had to be doing something to be of value because that's what I learned growing up.

A girl in my Sunday school class, Audrey, encouraged me to join the children's choir that practiced on Thursday evenings. We'd sing our hearts out at rehearsal sitting up in the theater style pews facing front center where Mr. Stevens played the organ, laughing and joking around in between songs.

Mr. Stevens pulled me aside one day and had me sing, "Let there be Peace on Earth," by myself. I did it, not thinking much about it and the next thing I knew I had my name in the following week's Church program. When Dad drove me to church that week in his sea blue suit and matching tie, I thought less about singing a solo in front of the whole congregation and more about why Dad decided to go to church, not connecting the two. My parents never attended my activities, events or school interviews so this was definitely out of character.

My parents put me in anything that interested me including swimming, judo, oil painting and baseball mostly to keep me busy, out of their hair and out of trouble. I liked the feeling of winning and the attention from Mom and Dad that came with it, so I welcomed the opportunity to stand out. My parents would prominently display my trophies on the living room coffee tables, and oil paintings on their walls even though they visibly clashed with the gold, red and black Spanish décor. When we had company, my parents would brag about me over

Rye and Cokes, and I would beam with pride and soak in their praises.

Unconsciously, I found a way to fill that shameful hole created by stealing from the Jongs and being blamed for the threat to blow them up. I needed to DO something great, like win a trophy, sing a solo or get sick to feel loved, and as an adult this belief continued to play out, masking itself in the roles I played. I felt anxiety about failing, not contributing or being of value to my family because I had the belief and was telling myself the story that, having MD prevented me from doing anything of value or doing something great.

The family role change was also evident when I was sitting in my van waiting for my children's bus to arrive near my ex partner's new house. In the rearview mirror, I noticed his girlfriend flip her long, black hair out from beneath her coat collar as she exited her front door. As she casually strolled toward the bus stop, I saw Maggie my dog at her side too. I thought, *"this woman is living my life. She has my partner, my children, my dog. She has my family. I've lost everything. My health, my family, even my dog."*

Ginger, my life coaching client, also struggled with a role change while experiencing marital problems and came to me to help her get her life back on track. She kept saying that she was broken. When we investigated her earlier memories, we uncovered the fact that as a child she felt broken when her father preferred the presence of her brother, and often dismissed or ignored her. As an adult, when her husband dismissed or ignored her, or her needs, she felt he didn't value her. This made her feel incredibly emotional and she had an overwhelming sense of being broken. Ginger re-experienced the brokenness from childhood mixed with the new brokenness of her marriage and blamed her husband for the experience. Ginger perceived that her role in the family was changing from being of value to not being valued, and it triggered her limiting belief that not being of value meant she was broken. Her husband was the tool being used to draw awareness to the crack in her foundation. That limiting belief needed attention before she moved forward so it would not create future problems.

Once we connected the limiting belief to the trigger, we were able to create a plan to find value just as she was, from within, rather than rely on outside circumstances that were unpredictable and continuously changing.

4. Leisure and community

It could be that you golfed, skied, canoed, acted, volunteered, danced or partied. Whatever the recreational or community activity, it can shape who you think you are.

What do the activities you love to do say about you? Are you active, fun, out-going, adventurous, spontaneous, fit, healthy, capable? Those characteristics often become attributed to you because of your participation in that activity or with that group. When prevented from doing all those activities, you can feel a sense of loss, or emptiness. It is not just the act of golfing that filled the void, it's all the other emotional, mental and physical benefits as well.

That's why you might find it so annoying when people say, "Just find something else to do that interests you." You're not just looking for an activity to fill the time; you're looking to get filled up emotionally, mentally and physically, the way you did with the old activity.

Let's take golf, for example, the fresh air, the physical exertion, the challenge, the social game, the growth, the after game drink and talk, the score, the time to yourself are what made you feel good. The relaxation, the fun, happiness, pride when you get a birdie, the power in your legs as you scaled the hill, the flexibility, the feeling of being athletic, fit, able, capable, strong, competitive, and talented are the feelings that you miss.

Bouncing back and finding your momentum again after experiencing a health challenge can't be done just by filling your time with activities to keep you busy. The key is to fill yourself up emotionally and mentally from within. Once you become aware of what you are missing and what the rewards are, you can use that knowledge to move forward.

5. Spiritual

Experiencing a health challenge or a loss can make us question our faith, spiritual beliefs, mortality and religious background. As a result, it changes who we think we are and how we show up in the world. This role can impact all other areas of our lives including the relationships we have in our families, in our friendships, and in our professions. This challenge may also transform you, and your spiritual beliefs.

If you have had a large role, and a strong connection to your faith and religious community, you may find that this new experience expands or alters what you previously believed to be true for you. It could strengthen your beliefs, or it might create more questions. Either way, the rewards or benefits that you used to get from your religious connections may change. This is not about judging this change as good or as bad; it's about taking notice. Our role, our spiritual role said something about us. We got something from it.

When I discovered my partner was having an affair, it broke me open. I reached out to Jen, a friend from University many times, trying to make sense of the chaos that followed me, the depression that smothered me and the life that beat me down. I yearned to understand why it was happening to me. "It has to be for a reason. There must be something I can do with all this pain besides suffer. What does God want me to do?" That was the crack where the *essence of who I really was,* poked through the foundation of my perceptions giving me a sense that there was something more. From there on in, people, books, and experiences drew me further and further inward as my foundation strengthened and the suffering lessened.

TAKING ON A NEW ROLE

When your identity is wrapped up in a role you play, and you can't play that role anymore, it can hurt. It hurts because when the role or **what you do** changes, so do all the emotional, mental or physical rewards. With this loss, you may find yourself grappling to form a new role to fill the emotional void inside created by the challenge and role changes.

What easier role for people experiencing a health crisis than the illness itself. The "I'm sick," role. I don't believe we consciously set out to play that role, but are driven by the urge to feel better, and slide into the role without realizing it. Our unconscious seeks to replace some of the emotional, mental and physical benefits of lost roles by tapping into old files of beliefs and thought patterns that netted the same results.

Unconsciously, I had an old file called " how to get help and feel relief." I heard the sound of airless coughing through the darkness in the middle of the night Mom's cancer got worse. She grappled to take each breath, and I waited and hoped the phlegm would release itself from her lungs to give her relief. It always reminded me that the cancer was ravishing her lungs and eating away at my life. The fits of coughing and the pain got worse. The prescription bottles began to claim the kitchen counter, and the morphine made it difficult for her to function especially in the evenings when it was time for her to take her medications. I began setting my clock to wake myself up and go to her room. Gently rousing her from her slumber, I ensured she took her pills. It started to take a toll, making it difficult for me to focus at school each day. I longed for the life of a teenager; to be carefree, selfish and lazy.

Mom was getting worse, and the morphine made her see things like bugs crawling on the carpet or sounds that only she could hear. Before I left for school, I saw Mom sitting in her chair with a cigarette hanging loosely from her two fingers with an inch-long ash, arched and strained from its tip. I wanted to take the cigarette and put it out, but I realized that cigarette was all she had. Emotionally I felt numb and physically, my body screamed. I had a jabbing pain that shot through my right shoulder blade like a twisted knife each time I moved and a headache that never went away.

I called my sister and pleaded, "I need some help. Mom is getting worse, and I can't do this by myself anymore." Leone had just had her first child, was on maternity leave and was able to come to Port Colborne and help me with Mom. The heavy burden lifted from my shoulders, letting me revert to being a teenager with no responsibilities. Death still hung in the air, but I escaped by leaving the house, which I did as often as I could. I had discovered that if someone was suffering enough, people would come and help.

Thoughts and belief patterns from our childhood can unknowingly shape our present day experiences and dictate our behaviors and emotions making it difficult to change. I had unknowingly believed that being sick would bring help and relief, and unconsciously played the role of being sick, seeking its emotional benefit to help deal with my illness. It was what I learned to be true and as a result, I was living my adult life accordingly.

In the same way, you might be taking on a new role without realizing it, such as the role of unemployed, divorced, single parent, widow, retired, broke, drinker, etc.

HOW TO IDENTIFY THAT YOU HAVE TAKEN ON A NEW ROLE?

A) You own it using the "I" statement.

I am disabled. I have cancer. I am ill. I have a heart condition. You introduce yourself and shortly after that, share your story. I am broke, I am unemployed, I am a single parent.

B) The new role consumes your day. Conversation, thoughts, activities and social connections all have to do with the new role.

My body ached from the time I woke up to the time I went back to bed and consumed my thoughts and experiences. I was either absorbed by the illness or, the thoughts of how to get rid of it. Either way, my days were filled with everything to do with my ill health.

C) Taking inventory of what you **can't** do consumes your daily life.

I can't go out because I have no money. I can't get ahead. I can't pay my bills. I can't.....

D) You live today with the assumption of a predetermined outcome.

Decisions and actions today are in consideration of a distant future experience. For example, "I have cancer, I am going to die, my life is over, and all activities of living cease, relationships fall away, dreams stop, joy ends. As my mother-in-law used to say, "I have stopped buying green bananas."

Let's assume you got a medical diagnosis of a chronic disease. Before your diagnosis, you had no idea whether or not you would live another day. You could have choked on a bone, got hit by a car or suffered a heart attack at any time but that never kept you from buying green bananas. Why? Because somewhere in your unconscious there was the belief that, that was not how you would die, and you went about your life without considering it. Your diagnosis, however, may have resulted in the creation of a new limiting, plausible outcome, one which you may be rearranging your life for, to meet it.

E) Acting more limited than you are to justify meeting the expectations of old or new roles.

When I first qualified for long term disability, I struggled with what I should and should not be doing because I had this standard in my mind of what "disabled" meant and I didn't match it. I believed unconsciously that someone who was disabled and unable to work should be at death's door, unable to feed themselves or go anywhere. If you had seen me park in a handicapped parking spot back then, you too may have questioned my need for the parking space. I looked fine based on outside appearances, but unbeknownst to passersby, I fatigued quickly and wore an ankle orthotic for foot drop. Sometimes to avoid their stares and judgment of strangers, I would add a little limp to my step as I walked into the store so as to meet their expectations of what someone should act like if they were handicapped.

F) Society and the new role.

Society often requires people to play the role of being sick. Doctors, insurance companies, employers, government disability programs, tax guidelines, financial support organizations and assistance programs continually request that you demonstrate and prove how sick you are for you to access their services. They repeatedly ask details about all the things that you can't do, the amount of pain or other physical problems that you endure and what aspects of your life you are incapable of performing. Access to benefits or services can be limited or completely unavailable if your responses are not considered to be that of someone who is completely disabled and unable to work, therefore encouraging people to exaggerate, emphasize and focus on how <u>bad</u> their life is. The same could be said for unemployment insurance and spousal support.

I believe our thoughts can have a profound impact on our experience, and if a person is required to rehearse and regurgitate how bad things are, then their experience will turn out to be just that. The role of sickness can ultimately make things worse. Societal expectations of a disabled person can demotivate and hinder their bid for wellness by requiring them to be as ill as possible, and, therefore, narrowing their perspective of possibilities. This certainly was true in my case. My life became a shadow of what it was before leaving my teaching job.

Every moment I had a choice to keep doing what I was doing or to do something differently. Either way, my end game was the same. I would die one day; everyone does, but the journey of how I would get there was up for grabs. I could have entertained a different way of experiencing those four years but my limited perception of what I thought was possible was so narrow it blocked out other experiences and possibilities. It was as though I was frozen in the experience, terrified of the future. If only I had known that everything would be more than OK. If only my wise self of today could write a letter to my terrified self fifteen years ago.

Dear Lori

This is a letter to you from your wise self fifteen years in the future. I want to hug you and let you know that you have everything you need within you to find the happiness you seek. You are an incredibly powerful being and what you accomplish in the next 15 years will absolutely blow your mind.

Soon, you will decide to move forward and do things differently by questioning your thoughts, challenging preconceived limits and walking through monumental fear to discover that nothing outside of yourself is necessary to obtain inner peace. All that is required of you, is to let go, relinquish control of what you think should happen in your life and allow all that you are to pour forth.

You believe your body has failed you but the fact is, it has saved you. Your journey inward will help you rediscover who you really are and deem you more capable than you ever thought possible.

My dearest Lori, you can choose to keep doing what you are doing, perceiving as you perceive and thinking as you are thinking and that's OK. This is your life, and you can't do it wrong. However, if you decide right now to **live your best life**, to enjoy the journey and open yourself up to the opportunities laid out before you, 15 years from now you will kneel down and lovingly thank your younger self.

Thank you for the ride.

Love Lori

WHO ARE YOU NOT?

Who are you if you are not the roles you play or the illness you have?

When you have an illness, or experience a loss, the outside, external reality (job, social life, the body, etc.) changes, but the inside, in your heart, who you are, stays the same. In that case, who are you?

Well, we know what you are not.

- You are not the work you do. You can lose a job or leave a job and still be you.
- You are not the sibling, son or daughter. You can lose your parents and still be you.
- You are not the culture you were raised in. You can move away to a different country and still be you.
- You are not the spouse. You can be divorced and still be you.
- You are not the parent or grandparent.
- You are not the golfer, yogi or dancer.
- You are not the volunteer.

Those may be all things that you do...but it is not who you are. I know this because I can take all those things away from you and **you...will still be you**! The real you! I was led to believe that my body and what I did made up who I was, but I have found that when my body can't do anything, I am still me. I am still in here. Rediscovering, who you really are is a little bit like, "Finding Waldo." If you strip away the distractions (the cracks in your foundation), you're left with a pure version of what you're looking for. You are still you, no matter what the diagnosis, condition or state. The only thing keeping you from knowing, feeling and believing that with all your heart, is your belief that you are what you do or the roles you play.

PRACTICE AND REFLECTION

Exercises to help rediscover who you really are.

1. What were the rewards or benefits you received from the following?

    A. Your job?

    B. Your friendships?

    C. Your family?

    D. Leisure/Community?

E. Spiritual/religious connections?

- Consider what emotional, mental or physical paybacks you may have been getting by having those roles.

- What expectations did you have of yourself and others? How have those expectations changed?

- How did these those roles contribute to your identity?

2. I want you to imagine that you are 100 years old. You are looking back on your life, and I want you to write down the five most important things *you would want people to remember about you.*

   A)

   B)

C)

D)

E)

3. Write the names of the 3 most important people in your life across the top. Answer the questions for each.

Questions	1.	2.	3.
A. If they could choose one quality to describe you, which one would **you** want them to choose			
B. If they used 3 words to describe you, what 3 words would **you** want them to choose?			
C. What would **you** want them to say is what they love most about having you in their life?			
D. If you could choose, the greatest impact you could have on them, what impact would **you** choose?			
E. What do you think will be their most favorite memory of **you**? Why?			
F. If they could spend 1 more day with you, how do you think they would like to spend it?			

4. The real you.

A) Review your answers to the previous questions and ask yourself,

a) What do you value most?

b) What do they value most?

c) Do you need a complete body, healthy or otherwise, money, security, etc. to experience those things?

B) Write "I am...." At the top of the page in your journal. Record the answers from question 3A, 3B, and 3C and read them aloud to yourself.

C) How do you feel before and after doing exercise 4A and 4B?

5. Feel the love

A) What could you do or say today, to one of the three people in Exercise #3 above, to show them that they are loved by you? Here are some examples of what you could say to them.

- I love you.
- I am proud of you.
- You did great.
- I'm glad I am your mom(dad).
- I adore you.
- You're amazing.
- Thank you.
- I couldn't imagine life without you.
- You're the best son (daughter).
- I admire you.
- I heart you.
- I care for you.
- I cherish you.
- Give them a hug.
- I enjoy spending time with you.
- Tell them about something they did that meant a lot to you.
- You make life fun.

- Tell me about your day.
- Remember when?
- Send a card.
- Saying you are my sunshine to someone.
- You are irreplaceable.
- You are a treasure.
- Text ILY (I Love You).
- Text U R GR8T.
- Give them a hug and a kiss.
- Tell them, "I love you more each day."

B) Find one thing today that you want from someone else and give it away. If you want affection, give affection to someone. If you want attention, give attention to someone.

6. What would your letter say from your wiser future self to your present day self? What do you want to see looking back at your life? Do you want to remember how you white knuckled it, put on the brakes and gritted your teeth all those years or smiled, laughed and enjoyed the ride?

Speak the words you long to hear by inserting your name in each of the spaces below and read the letter out loud. Reflect on the letter after you read it, and record your thoughts and insights.

Dear _____

This is a letter to you from your wise self fifteen years in the future. I want to hug you and let you know that you have everything you need within you to find the happiness you seek. You are an incredibly powerful being and what you accomplish in the next 15 years will absolutely blow your mind.

Soon, you will decide to move forward and do things differently by questioning your thoughts, challenging preconceived limits and walking through monumental fear to discover that nothing outside of yourself is necessary to obtain inner peace. All that is required of you is to let go, relinquish control of what you think should happen in your life and allow all that you are to pour forth.

You believe your life has failed you but the fact is, it has saved you. Your journey inward will help you rediscover who you really are and deem you more capable than you ever thought possible.

My dearest _____, you can choose to keep doing what you are doing, perceiving as you perceive and thinking as you are thinking and that's OK. This is your life, and you can't do it wrong. However, if you decide right now to live your best life, to enjoy the journey and open yourself up to the opportunities laid out before you, 15 years from now you will kneel down and lovingly thank your younger self.

Thank you for the ride.

Love _____

CHAPTER SIX: ATTACHMENT AND EXPECTATION

What dream do you have? Do you want to work until you're fifty, retire and do some traveling? Maybe buy a retirement home in Florida, a cottage on the lake or take cruises every couple years? Perhaps you would prefer staying close to home and play bingo Friday nights or golf every day? Do you expect to live to the age of ninety-nine and then die in your sleep just before you get so old you can't have fun anymore?

There is nothing wrong with dreaming. It is motivating, exciting, and gives you something to look forward to, promotes change, growth and creates an interest in what's to come. Dreaming can also help to formulate goals, develop new skills, empower and motivate you to move forward in your life.

When you invest in a vision of the future and reality matches it, it feels great, but when reality does not meet your expectations of the future, as when you are diagnosed with an illness or experience a loss, it can have a profound effect on your emotional, mental, physical and spiritual well-being.

The dream I had of my future crumbled and threw me into a whirlwind of grief the minute I got diagnosed with the muscle disorder. I grieved the life I wanted, the life I would never have, grieved the horrible life that awaited me and grieved having to grieve!

EXPECTATION

The Wikipedia definition of expectation is

"In the case of uncertainty, expectation is what is considered the most likely to happen. An expectation, which is a belief that is centered on the future, may or may not be realistic. A less advantageous result gives rise to the emotion of disappointment. If something happens that is not at all expected; it is a surprise."

When we face a challenge like an illness, it threatens the dream or vision that we have for our lives. We are not only grieving what is tangibly affected by the disease or disability, but we are also grieving everything in our dreams that we may no longer be able to do. We grieve all the things that we were expecting to do in the future.

Let's be clear. When we invest in our vision of the future and reality matches it, meaning, everything you want comes to you...it's fantastic. Again, I am not suggesting that we not dream, think big and desire all that the world has to offer. What I am suggesting, however, is that we dream big and let go of attachment to the outcome because if we don't, it can have a profound effect on our emotional, mental, physical and spiritual well-being when things don't work out as planned.

How do we become so invested in our life plan? It's kind of like money. Our life is like a currency and it holds value. And just like money, when we invest it, we expect a return. The more we invest, the bigger return we expect. If it works out, the bigger the payoff; if it doesn't, the greater the loss.

4 DIFFERENT WAYS YOU INVEST IN YOUR DREAMS

1. Emotional Investment
2. Mental Investment
3. Physical Investment
4. Spiritual Investment

1. Emotional investment

This happens when you anticipate an experience and the positive emotions attached to it. You imagine a future, create an expectation of what it will be like emotionally for you to have it, and then wait for its arrival.

A vacation is an example of a positive emotional investment. Visions of cold, refreshing Pina Coladas, vibrant sunsets, and moonlit dinners occupy your thoughts, and feelings of excitement, relaxation and pleasure warm your insides even before you reach the airport. You begin investing emotionally in the experience before it happens, and you do the same thing with your life. You project what your future will look and feel like, long before you actually experience it.

If you experience an illness, relationship change, job loss or financial challenge it can give rise to disappointment because your positive expectation or dreams can appear to be no longer possible and the life you wanted can feel like a death or emotional loss.

You can have a negative expectation of your future too. A negative projection of a life unwanted can be as vividly imagined as the vacation experience described above, and can create the emotions and feelings of that vision as though they were happening right now. You imagine the struggles, pain, and challenges that manifest as fear in the moment. It's all imagined but feels very real.

Byron Katie (2007) said, "Fear has only two causes: the thought of losing what you have or the thought of not getting what you want" (p. 175). These two fears are rooted in expectation. You expect things to stay the same, the comfort of what is familiar, and you expect your future to be as you imagined, or what you want.

One of the most difficult times in my life was when my partner asked for a divorce. I had never considered it to be a possibility that I would not be married to the same person for the rest of my life. I envisioned watching our children have children and sharing in their lives together. I was invested emotionally in the idea of growing old, loving each other to the very end and being married to the same person for the rest of my life. When that did not happen, I realized that I grieved the loss of my partner, but grieved even more, the loss of my marriage and the expectation of all that I wanted it to be.

Have you heard the expression, "finding your passion?" The underlying belief is that everyone has something here on earth that they were destined to do and when they find it, they'll be happy. That is a form of emotional investment or expectation. I remember thinking that if I could just find my passion, that thing that I was born to do, I would be happy. It excited me to think that there was something out there that I was meant to do; that fit my interests, my skills and would bring me joy. It also terrified me too. What if I go through life and never find it?

My desire to find my passion was rooted in my belief that, "finding my passion," would make me feel a certain way. I was investing in the idea that if I found it, I would be happy. What I was really looking for was something outside myself to trigger positive, passionate and loving thoughts and emotions within me.

Why is having an emotional investment a problem? It is a problem because it makes happiness a moving target. Think of a time when you were disappointed. Why were you disappointed? You had an expectation of how things were going to go and how it would make you feel, and it didn't turn out that way. You were invested in something outside yourself to make you feel happy. The problem with that strategy is that everything outside yourself is destined to change.

2. Mentally Invested

Our thoughts, beliefs, and images regarding our future are logically and linearly structured creating a false sense of predictability and control. Our mind loves structure, order, and predictability because responding automatically requires less effort. Varying from this structure of thought requires change and change requires developing new ways of doing things. "It takes more effort to think about and do something new than react out of instinct or habit (Langley, 2012)."

Recently a video from Smartereveryday.com was circulating the Internet about a gentleman trying to ride a backward bike. When he turned the handlebars to the right, the front wheel turned left, and when he turned the handlebars to the left, the front wheel turned to the right. As a result of this modification, he was unable to ride the bike and others had the same difficulty. What was so fascinating about this, was that the ingrained behavior of riding a regular bike initially prevented the rider from learning a new way to behave or respond to a similar situation, which was riding a different bike.

It took this gentleman weeks to learn to ride the backward bike, and he admitted that if he were distracted or lost focus, he would immediately fall back into old habits and lose his balance. This is an amazing example of how our unconscious mind dictates our responses by default making it challenging to change.

Most of the time, your unconscious mind allows you to perform multiple tasks by default so that you don't have to focus on each particular task. This is incredibly helpful when driving a car, walking or scratching your nose.

Can you imagine what it would be like if you had to consciously decide about every response? Scratching your nose would become an all-consuming activity. You would have to choose the finger, the arm it is attached to, calculate the height and angle of movement, place the finger strategically near the itch, put it gently on the skin, focus on bending the finger, then straightening out, and so on, just to satisfy an itch!

Your brain is incredible at taking in new experiences and filing them away into neat, condensed folders of similar design. Once you know how to scratch your nose, your brain generalizes and responds similarly to situations requiring the same need, like itching your knee or face.

It can be difficult to make changes to your thinking when the unconscious mind generalizes and responds based on outdated folders in your mind.

When your third-grade teacher told you, "you're not good at math," that may have stuck with you, in your math folder, in your memories. Now as an adult, you may find yourself avoiding your personal finances, unaware as to why you hate doing it so much. Your unconscious may have generalized that math or working with numbers is related to that sickening feeling you got in third-grade math class. It didn't feel good so now; you avoid anything like mathematics to avoid feeling bad. This outdated program remains active and utilized by your unconscious mind even though you may be very competent dealing with numbers.

Because we act and behave based on learned behaviors and belief systems, we become mentally invested in what we already know and believe. It is easier on your brain.

For the third-grade student to change and stop avoiding mathematical situations, he would have to indulge in mathematical experiences over and over again, allowing him opportunities to gain confidence (new positive belief folder) along the way and creating a strong, positive feeling (creating an emotional charge). When the third grader gets used to "feeling good" around math, chances are he will more likely recognize when the old habitual behavior seeps in. Becoming aware when the old default behavior creeps up, allows the individual to bring the experience to the conscious mind and, therefore, to allow for choice. A choice as to how they will respond. To avoid the mathematical situation or engage it.

If you are getting frustrated about making a change, I want you to appreciate the power of learned behavior and beliefs, and the steps it takes to change a deep seeded pattern. That's why your mind is screaming for your body to heal, or demanding the return of a partner that loves someone else. Your mind wants everything to go back to the way it was. It wants you to be doing what you have always done and to dream what you have always dreamed because it is easier that way. Your mind believes that the old way is the only path to happiness and is keeping you focused on that single perspective. It believes that holding on to the past will bring relief but in fact, the opposite is true. The resistance to change is the actual cause of stress. Therefore, by resisting change, the mind is keeping you in a perpetual state of stress.

In, *The Neuroscience of Change: Why it's difficult and what makes it easier*, Langley (2012) stated, "we are inclined to avoid what seems threatening, rather than embrace it. We feel uncertain, focus on the negative and disengage. Our prefrontal cortex also has less reserves of energy (oxygen and glucose) so we are less likely to make good decisions, take on new ideas, create new dreams, adapt old ones or experience gratitude. When we feel threatened...we are inclined to do whatever it takes to get rid of it, rather than embrace it, and move forward."

3. Physically Invested

The physical body you imagine in your future, may be set in expectation. You can become attached to all the things related to the body's performance including its ability to carry out the physical aspects of your dreams. Consider the idea that many have of retiring and spending days on the golf course. That vision requires a healthy and capable body to do so. When the body breaks down, the whole dream appears to break down too.

Langley (2012) suggests our brain is physically wired to avoid change. "To keep it simple we often use the triune brain analogy. The triune brain has three parts: the reptilian brain which is responsible for our primary drivers such as eating, sleeping and sex; the limbic system which includes our emotions, connection with others, memory and habits; the pre-frontal cortex which is responsible for higher order thinking. The pre-frontal cortex takes more energy to function whereas the limbic system is energy efficient. What that means is it takes more effort to think about and do something new than react out of instinct or habit." Your body is wired not to change because it takes less effort to keep things the same. It is physically invested in maintaining the status quo.

The financial wellness of your future may appear dependent on your body's ability to work and earn money. Experiencing a health challenge or job loss can threaten your perceived ability to take care of basic needs, familial obligations and investments for retirement. When a health crisis strikes, you may also fear that you will not be able to care for yourself in the future.

I exchanged one expectation for another. First, I was unable to work as a teacher, and financially contribute to my family, which left me scared and anxious. I was relieved when I started receiving disability support payments but my attachment to this funding source to take care of my needs was just as powerful. I was always concerned about the possibility that they would cancel my payments, imagining worst case scenarios of not being able to support myself. My physical body was connected to my emotional investment in financial security because I was counting on my disability payments to secure my future financial needs.

4. Spiritually Invested

You may be invested in underlying spiritual beliefs like, if you are "Good," good things will happen to you or that if you think positively you will be protected and avert future discomfort or challenges. When this doesn't happen, and adversity does occur, it can shake your faith and belief systems too.

EXCHANGING ONE EXPECTATION FOR ANOTHER

The interesting thing about an illness or disability is that it can permanently change your dreams and reveal your attachments. Inside, you haven't changed, you still want what you want, but your body has somehow dropped the ball so to speak. It is no longer holding up its end of the bargain.

When I was no longer working, I wanted to hold onto my dreams, make everything go back to the way it used to be and prayed for a cure. I wanted my dreams. They were **my** dreams. But the attachment I had to want what I wanted, left me exhausted and depleted. Instead of being open to change or imagine the possibility that great things were possible for me regardless of the diagnosis, I could only entertain the thoughts that without my original plans, life was not worth living.

After deciding to think positively, eliminate old belief patterns and create new dreams, I fell hard when the MD progressed. I slid backward because I exchanged one expectation for another. I exchanged the expectation of having a healthy body to fulfill my dreams to be happy, with the expectation that my body would heal and be healthy again. Both were conditions outside of myself that had to change to make me happy. For me to be happy, reality needed to match what I wanted, and it didn't.

I had experienced a pattern of emotional, mental, physical, spiritual investment and expectation each time the disease plateaued and then, disappointment each time the disease progressed. This pattern illuminated the unreasonable search of happiness in outside circumstances. The pursuit was futile, because true happiness has to come from within.

The Law of Attraction indicated that I needed to love what I have. How can I love what I have and at the same time, want something different? If I truly loved what I had, I wouldn't want something different, and if I didn't want anything different, I wouldn't have any expectations. If I didn't have any expectations, I would love everything, just as it is, and would be happy in the moment regardless of outside circumstances.

EXPECTATIONS TRANSFORMED

Let's go back to the definition of expectation which it says, *"expectation is what is considered the most likely to happen."*

You may have an expectation of a future that you consider most likely to occur, but if you become attached to that expectation, and it becomes the benchmark for your happiness it can potentially set you up for suffering.

How can you work towards a goal or dream without becoming attached? Having a goal or vision is like using a GPS in your car. You punch in where you want to go, but the GPS focuses on where you are now and the first part of the journey. The end point is not even on the screen. You can do the same thing with your goal or vision by breaking it down into smaller steps, and then decide what would be the first logical action you could take to move forward, shifting your focus to the present moment.

Life is not about the end game, the tomorrows or what you'll get when. It's about the journey of today each transforming moment at a time. As you become more and more present in the moment, new possibilities and opportunities become visible. You become more flexible to make changes too because you're not stuck on one single outcome. As a result, the chance to gain valuable skills, meet different people and expand beyond perceived limitations becomes possible. Change your future expectation to a moment to moment awareness and experience, and you'll move from disappointment to openness and possibility.

FINDING HAPPINESS BY TRANSFORMING EXPECTATIONS

I had a coaching client named Cathy, who had an expectation of what she wanted her relationship to be like. She had determined that if her mate were more positive, outgoing and loving her marriage would be everything she had hoped it would be. Cathy's expectation and projection of what her husband needed to do differently, were the tools she could use to find happiness. We discovered that Cathy felt her husband was unloving, negative and boring. He was mirroring what Cathy was resisting within herself and she needed to explore where in her life she was, or had been unloving, negative and boring (Using Exercise 3 in Practice and reflection from Chapter 3). Secondly, we created a plan together to help Cathy elicit the desired feelings of love, positivity and excitement today, using the 5 Steps to Experience Your Dream Today found in the Practice and Reflection below.

PRACTICE AND REFLECTION

What if being happy requires nothing outside of yourself and you have the means to be that right now?

5 Steps to Experience Your Dream Today

1. Dream with detail.

2. Identify desired emotions.

3. Create an Emotional Vision Board.

4. Act to elicit the emotions.

5. Dream big, with detail and emotion. Then, let the dream go.

It's not the people, the experiences or the things that get you to feel a certain way but the thoughts and beliefs you have about them. By following the **5 Steps to experience your dream today,** you'll be able to experience <u>now</u> what you only dreamed of experiencing in the <u>future.</u>

1. Dream and describe the dream in as much detail as possible

It's important to get familiar with your vision, so familiar in fact, that if you were to tell someone about it, they would feel like they were right there with you. Answer the following questions to explore your dream in detail. Let's take a look at an example in the table below. Let's suppose you have a dream of being loved.

Questions about your dream, vision or goal	Answer	Feelings and emotions associated with each
In your dream, when you are being loved, who is there?		
In your dream while being loved, what are you doing?		
Where are you being loved?		
What does, "being loved," look like?		
Time of year? Time of Day? What can you see near you, far away?		
What are you wearing in your dream?		

Continued on next page

Questions about your dream, vision or goal	Answer	Feelings and emotions associated with each
In your dream while being loved, what are you feeling? Physically? Emotionally? Mentally?		
What are you getting from this experience of being loved? What other emotions are rising within you?		
Who else is affected by you being loved? Colleagues, family, friends?		
Being loved and going about your day. What does your day look like? Walk through it from morning until night.		
In this dream of being loved, when you wake up in the morning, tell me what you're thinking.		
In this dream of being loved, when you get into bed, and pull the covers up under your chin, what goes through your mind?		

2. Now that we have explored the expectations we may have of the dream, "Being loved, " I want us to explore the feelings that might be attached to these visions. Some of the questions in number one, asked about feelings directly, and those can be copied right into the third column.

Questions about your dream, vision or goal.	Answer	Feelings and Emotions Associated with each
In your dream, when you are being loved, who is there?	*Significant other, tall dark and handsome*	*Excited, happy*
In your dream while being loved, what are you doing?	*Hanging out together, sharing thoughts, daily happenings*	*Connected, close, playful*
Where are you being loved?	*At home, on walks outside*	*Comforted, content*

Here are some emotionally descriptive words to help illustrate the feelings attached to a dream or goal.

Open, understanding, confident, reliable, easy, amazed, free, sympathetic, interested, satisfied, receptive, accepting, kind, great, gay, joyous, lucky, fortunate, delighted, overjoyed, gleeful, thankful, important, festive, ecstatic, satisfied, glad, cheerful, sunny, merry, elated, playful, courageous, energetic, liberated, optimistic, provocative, impulsive, frisky, spirited, thrilled, wonderful, animated, calm, peaceful, at ease, comfortable, pleasing, encouraged, clever, surprised, quiet, certain, relaxed, serene, bright, blessed, loving, considerate, affectionate, sensitive, tender, devoted, attracted, passionate, admiration, warm, touched, sympathy, close, loved, comforted, concerned, affected, fascinated, intrigued, absorbed, inquisitive, engrossed, curious, eager, keen, intent, inspired, determined, bold, daring, challenged, optimistic, confident, hopeful, impulsive, dynamic, tenacious, secure, surprising amused, appreciative, enjoyable, euphoric, excellent, exultant, fabulous, blissful, bouncy, faithful, fortunate, fun, lucky, magnificent, marvelous, outstanding, peaceful, pleasant, pleasurable, cherry, witty, comfortable, content, dedicated, glad, glorious, gracious, grateful, great, happy, honorable, inspirational, positive, proud, respectable, sincere, splendid, superb, terrific, tremendous, triumphant

3. Emotional Vision Board

With this list, I would encourage you to create an **Emotional Vision Board**. This is different from an ordinary vision board because a regular vision board usually illustrates photos or experiences, relationships or physical things that people desire, have or do.

A DAILY Emotional or Feeling Vision Board uses words or pictures to represent the **feelings** associated with the dream experience, relationship or physical object.

If you don't have the time to complete the vision board now, I invite you to keep the list to the right, under the heading, **"Feelings and Emotions Associated with each,"** visible.

Next, on the same piece of paper or a new one, I want you to put the word, **Love**, right there in the middle representing our Dream of "being Loved." Looking at the list of things you wrote down about the dream of being loved, I want you to select 5 or six that stand out to you, and record them around the word, "Love," that you wrote down in the middle of the page.

4. Emotionally Charged Action

Next, brainstorm, all the things you could do today to feel those feelings. No judgment here. Just write down whatever comes to you. Remember, things you can do today. Not tomorrow, but today. What can you do today that would elicit the feeling of being excited? Connected? Playful?

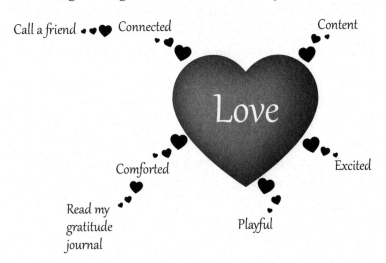

5. Dream Big and let go.

Next, dream. Dream big and add to your Emotional Vision Board (EVB). Dream large and often and let go. Let it go? What does that mean? It means send it off, into the ether; the sky whatever works for you, but let it go. Know inside that it requires no other focus or attention from you because you are working to get there with your daily actions. By creating experiences every day that elicit the emotions you desire, you are creating the future you're craving, right now, no matter how it shows up. The future of today and every day fills with the feelings and emotions you were hoping to experience later on.

Remember, it's not the dream relationship, experience or physical things we desire that are important, as much as it is the investment we have in it, what we believe we will also get from having it, and the emotions or feelings attached to it.

Life is about each transforming moment at a time. It's the journey of today. Change your future expectation, to a moment by moment awareness and experience, and you'll move from disappointment to openness and possibility by living your dream of happiness today.

CHAPTER SEVEN: POLARITY OF PERCEPTION

I was at a doctor's office having a routine exam, desperately expressing all the challenges I was having. "I can't roll over or rise from a chair anymore, and I struggle with balance and walking too." My doctor graciously listened and made some suggestions, but her words found nowhere to land. They were unsatisfying and not what I wanted to hear.

What could she say? I was stuck rehearsing how sick I was, and not looking for solutions. I was looking for everything to go back to the way it was. I wanted someone to make everything OK.

The doctor couldn't give me what I wanted, and shockingly, she said what I needed to hear instead. "You need to learn to deal with it."

What? I was completely stunned. *How dare she. How insensitive of her. Must be nice to be healthy, sitting there telling her patients to suck it up.* I felt my face burn red, my heart beat faster and tears rose, forming on my lower lid. My mind raced with replies to defend myself and then, in a split second, it all stopped. A gentle calm rose up within me and deep down, I felt her words land deep inside to a place of truth. I did need to suck it up and deal with it.

Now, don't get me wrong. I had another choice. I could have kept doing what I was doing, rehearsing how sick I was, telling myself and others how things should be different, that it shouldn't have happened to me, that it was unfair and so on and so forth. The thing was, though, every time I indulged in that, "storytelling," of my illness, it never made me feel any better. It was like climbing a hill and never getting a good grip but just grasping and slipping with every step. I never got the satisfaction of feeling relief, and it was exhausting.

At that moment when the doctor said, "You need to learn to deal with it, "I could actually, authentically hear her and I realized what I was doing was not working. I needed to do something differently. It was then that my perspective of the experience opened up a tiny bit and considered that there might be another way.

It's a matter of perspective

Recently, I parked my van at an angle and took up two parking spots. I did this because the only way for me to access my van is through the side door. Disability parking spots frequently do not have the extra space on the side of the vehicle for my ramp to deploy and for me to exit, so sometimes I take two regular parking spots. If I don't do that, people will often park too close, blocking me from getting in and making me wait until they return for me to be able to leave. It's not ideal taking two spots, but it works, most of the time.

The other day I noticed a napkin tucked under my windshield wiper. I thought, "Cool," someone must have seen my van, knew it was mine and left me a note to say hi. I wondered who it may have been, maybe Roy, Denise or Jamie? Excitedly, I reached up, grabbed the napkin and read, "You have won the Asshole Parking Award." Not what I expected. Clearly we had two different perspectives on my parking strategy.

The fact was I took up two spots. My experience of taking two spots and the award giver's experience of me taking two spots were entirely different. The one reality was that the van indeed straddled two spots. There were two perspectives of my parking job, and both perspectives were just as plausible. Had my napkin award giver opened herself up to one or maybe a few other reasons why someone might park at an angle, she might have saved herself the aggravation. I, on the other hand, opened myself to her perspective and could appreciate her special award because, in the past, I too have criticized people on their parking skills.

It is what it is. In this moment, it is what it is. Reality is exactly that, and then it is something else. We can't control the world outside of us but what we can control, is how we respond to reality. Let's take an illness for example. Whether we like it or not, we are going through the experience of a change in health. Today, right now, in this moment, the moment you are reading this, your health, is what it is. Wanting it to be different in this moment is like asking it to be sunny when it's raining, or to be ice skating on a tropical beach. In this moment, we can't change our health but what we can change, is how we experience it, how we react to it. Either way, this change in our health is happening. So how do you want to go through it?

We have all heard the expressions, "see the glass half full instead of half empty" or "when the world gives you lemons, make lemonade." What those expressions are suggesting is that in any particular situation, we have a choice as to how we see it.

I used to laugh at how the people who were always seeing the glass half full, seemed to have a perfect life and if you are like me, positive, happy people drove me crazy. I wanted to yell at them, "let's see how happy you'd be if you had to go through what I am going through." It seemed like an insurmountable task to see the positives in my day when the negatives completely blinded me. No matter how bright the other side of life was, I just couldn't see it. I didn't want to see it. I resisted. But why?

Why do we get locked into a single, negative perspective or response?

5 REASONS YOU GET STUCK IN A SINGLE PERSPECTIVE

1. There is a reward.

You are getting something, a payback by staying where you are. If you weren't, you wouldn't be doing it. The reward could be positive or negative but in any case, it is a payback all the same. For me, I believe seeing only one perspective kept me from having to change. I did not want to accept my life the way it was. I did not want to give up my mantra, that it should not be happening and the illness needed to go away.

Some people have suggested that I have created the illness with my thinking so I wouldn't have to work and could receive disability payments. I do not believe that people choose to be sick just as I don't believe people choose to age. I don't know whether or not my body will heal. It might heal. It might heal if my thoughts change, and it might heal if my thoughts don't change. What I have found that works is that if what I am thinking or doing feels right, good, in alignment with the core of who I am, then I think it and do it. If it does not feel good, I question it and consider a different choice. **Being aware of the emotional charge is the key to uncovering limiting beliefs, creating choice and supporting your movement forward.**

2. It's easier to blame everyone and everything

Blaming everything outside yourself for your unhappiness is easier than making the intrinsic changes within. As long as I blamed the disease, I was not required to do anything about it. I didn't have to take responsibility for my happiness, thoughts or beliefs.

3. Wanting to be in control

To accept or surrender to your experience means you're not in control.

Are you really in control though? Or do you feel <u>in control</u> only when your outside experiences are a match to what you want, and then feel <u>not in control,</u> when outside experiences don't match what you want? What if you could "want," everything in your experience? What if your perspective of everything was that you have everything you want and everything you need? Then, there would be no need for control.

4. Believing you can't be happy with any other perspective

You believe that you cannot be happy unless you are completely healthy. You think your body needs to be a certain way, your bank account needs a certain balance, or your relationship needs to be a certain way for you to have a happy life.

When you live with the belief that your outside circumstances create your happiness, you are always vulnerable to becoming unhappy because everything outside of you changes. Aging for example. You are one second older, every second. You'll never get that second back, and it will never be the same. You'll never experience that age again. Your body has aged, cells have died, and some have regenerated because your body is constantly changing. If you believe relationships, activities, jobs and healthy physical bodies make you happy, then when something happens to any one of these extrinsic experiences, you can fall apart.

Opening up to new perspectives allows you to see the gifts and possibilities that are otherwise hidden by limited focus. Think about the old expression, "You can't see the forest for the trees," for example. If you are zeroed in on only one perspective, all other possibilities are unavailable to you unless you back up, get away from the situation and entertain other ways of seeing it. If you practice finding the gifts in the moment, this can become your default response in all cases, revealing the happiness within you.

I have had clients come to me wanting to find their passion, the "thing," that will bring them joy because they believe that once they find their passion, they'll be happy. Instead of working with clients to find the "thing," I question them about how they think they'll feel when they find their passion and what that would mean to them. It's the feeling they want, not the thing. Once we know how they want to feel, we can create a plan together to elicit that feeling within them now, in everything they do.

It's not <u>what</u> you are experiencing that is bringing you joy, but your perception of it that brings you joy. When you connect with who you really are, the job, the body, the income, etc. is no longer required to experience inner joy.

5. A limiting belief -Fear

As previously learned, an unconscious belief may be operating in the present moment without you realizing it. Unknown fears or limiting beliefs may be keeping you from seeing other perspectives and other ways that you could be moving forward in your life. Any stress or fear that is arising within you indicates that a thought or belief is limiting your possibilities and obstructing solutions within that moment.

When I was 20 years old and diagnosed with muscular dystrophy, I was overwhelmed and very depressed. I was seeing a campus psychologist to help me deal with the news when she kept suggesting that I ask for help from my family and friends, but I refused.

"Why don't you call them?"

"I don't want them to be sad."

"Why not?"

I didn't have an explanation, but I knew deep inside that I should not reach out to them and under no circumstances would I be a burden. About 20 years later, I struggled with that same feeling because of my disability and physical limitations, and I was worried that my partner would leave me if I required too much help. That day came when he said, "I want a divorce. I can't handle you being disabled." This was more evidence to fuel the belief that if I ask for help, people will leave me, and it kept me paralyzed and afraid of moving forward in my life.

When Mom was dying of cancer, she loved having company. When visitors came by she would often ask them to do menial tasks for her like change a light bulb or kill a spider because she liked having people take care of things for her like Dad used to do. Eventually, people thought my Mom didn't want to visit with them but only wanted their help with household chores, so they stopped coming by. No one said that's why they stopped coming by, but unconsciously, that's what I believed to be true.

A narrow perspective was created within me, whether it was true or not, that if I asked people for help, they would leave me. Stress overwhelmed me every time I put myself in a position where I might have to ask people for assistance. On the outside, people saw the confident, independent Lori that grew up on Merritt Parkway but inside, I stood paralyzed, afraid to make a move that could leave me vulnerable and needing help. The muscular dystrophy magnified this potential need, triggering me, and created a constant state of tension every day. Not only was I dealing with the stress of the diagnosis and living with the consequences of having limited mobility but I was also dealing with the belief that if I asked anyone for help, they would leave me. Whenever presented with an opportunity, I would unconsciously predict whether or not I would have to ask for help if I chose to pursue it. If the opportunity made me vulnerable and in the need of help, I would ignore it and make excuses about how it was not right for me.

POLARITY OF PERSPECTIVE

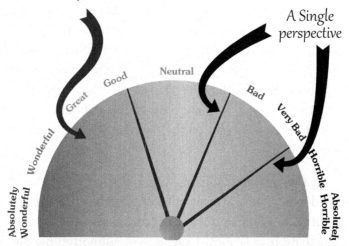

Infinite
Possibilities, Perceptions
or Reality

A Single
perspective

Neutral

Good

Great

Bad

Wonderful

Very Bad

Absolutely
Wonderful

Horrible

Absolutely
Horrible

Let's suppose that the shaded area in the diagram above represents all of the infinite possibilities or perceptions available to us at any given moment. In the moment, we experience one of those possibilities (represented in the above diagram as a straight single black line), and we have a perception (response) of that experience (wonderful, horrible, neutral).

Reality is what it is. You can't change that moment; it has already happened, and the shaded area represents that. That's the experience.

In every moment, we have the opportunity to see that moment in an infinite number of ways. Some perceptions feel good, some interpretations feel bad, and some interpretations may just feel neutral. Regardless of how we perceive it, the bottom line is that the moment is what it is. It's the same either way. So it is not the moment or the experience that is making you feel bad, good or neutral, but your perception of it.

I ran into a friend recently who I hadn't seen in about five years. After our initial chit chat, he said as he looked at me sitting in my power wheelchair, "you've lost some mobility."

"Actually, I gained mobility," I replied. We had two very different perspectives of the same reality, and both were absolutely true. If I chose to see my experience as he did, I would understand that being in a wheelchair limited my ability to move in life. I could totally identify with that. I had thousands and thousands of thoughts in my life that supported that view. In the past, I had had colossal fears of being in a wheelchair. I, too, once believed that being in a wheelchair limited one's mobility.

In that moment talking with my friend, however, I perceived being in a wheelchair completely differently. I saw how it allowed me to travel great distances, attend events and participate in activities. I saw how it supported me and met my needs. I saw how in reality it increased my mobility. A real blessing.

I believe we can get stuck when we only entertain one or two possible perceptions of our experiences. When our experiences are stressful or become fearful we close off to all of the other marvelous perceptions available to us regarding that same moment. Even if we had a neutral experience, the opportunity to perceive it as wonderful and perfect is always available to us, if you choose to see it that way. So why don't we?

Unconsciously, the mass of learned thoughts and beliefs that have created thousands of perceptions about thousands of things keep us seeing life the same way. When reality shows up to be similar to experiences we have had in the past, the more rigid our perception of the present event or experience becomes. Why? Because we have so much evidence in our memories to support it. For example, if I hear from a friend that Joe is arrogant and unkind, chances are my perception of Joe will be narrower on the polarity of perception scale than it would have been if I had never heard of Joe before. If when I meet Joe, I too see arrogance, my perception of Joe will narrow again. Joe may not be arrogant at all. Maybe he is confident, skilled and loving, but my perception of him will most likely be that he is arrogant because I have two examples from my experience to back it up. It's not right or wrong; he may be arrogant or not arrogant, it is just a perception.

Consciously, you can choose a different perception that is just as true because the reality of the moment doesn't change. You have to open yourself up to the other perceptions that are available to you and solidify them with an example in your life of how it is true. It might be that Joe is feeling unsure or trying hard to fit in. Maybe he's not arrogant at all but thinks that by talking about what he knows, he'll fit in with the group.

I was actively challenging myself to open up to different perspectives especially during chaotic, awful experiences. One day while working in the kitchen, I lost my balance and fell. Lying on the ceramic tile, looking up at the ceiling, I felt the tears well up and the throbbing of my knee and hip from where I hit the ground. I noticed my habitual, fearful reaction rising and right then and there, I chose to react differently.

"Everything is for me; I have everything I need in this moment. This is a gift. Find the gift in falling," I said out loud. I doubted at first that I would find anything to be grateful for as examples of doom and gloom crowded in, but when I looked around, I noticed that I had never really seen my kitchen from that view point before, and it really was interesting. I saw some dirt on the kick plate of my kitchen cupboards and thought, oh, now I can clean that. I reached into the cabinet and grabbed a cloth, wiped away the splatter while realizing I wouldn't have been able to do that, had I not fallen. I chuckled to myself. I felt the cool floor supporting me, and I stretched out, something I wouldn't normally have been able to do. I kept doing it until my energy shifted, changed from fear to neutral. Then, in a state of neutral, I identified my options to get myself standing and followed through with them, calmly and peacefully.

One perspective of my falling created a scared, panic, stressful journey to standing up again and the other view created a calm and peaceful journey to standing up again. Both were totally possible, neither one more right or more wrong, just different. The reality of it was that I fell and was lying on the ground. My future experience of standing could be experienced in many ways and in that moment, I chose to experience it with calm and peace.

HINDSIGHT IS 20/20

Have you ever looked back on an experience that you thought was devastating at the time but in hindsight, you could see how it was absolutely perfect? Can you think of a time when something horrible occurred, and in that moment you couldn't imagine how you were ever going to handle it, but then it ended up turning out to be one of the best things that ever happened to you? Oprah Winfrey often talked about how a conflict at work turned out to be the push she needed for a change in career and Wayne Dyer talked about being an orphan and how that experience helped him to become the man he was. They didn't see the gifts while these experiences were going on but the gifts were there, whether they noticed them or not.

It is possible to have the gift of hindsight by consciously choosing to see the gifts in every experience. Our freedom comes from opening up our perception of reality to the gifts in each moment and consciously making the effort to do so. We can do the same thing with past, negative memories too. You can't change what happened to you, but you can change your perception of it.

You can go through this challenge rehearsing and story-telling with great detail about how bad it is. And it will be true. You can go through this challenge repeating and storytelling with great detail about how great it is. And it will be true.

As William Shakespeare said, "There is nothing good or bad, but thinking makes it so."

PRACTICE AND REFLECTION

Let's practice. Let us assume that for each of the following three scenarios that your perception lies close to the right-hand side of the perception diagram, illustrating that you perceive the situation as absolutely horrible and see only the devastating effects of the experience. Your goal here is to move that needle, anywhere to the left, seeing a new and more positive perspective of the situation.

A) You lose your job. Some different perspectives of losing your job may include that you can spend more time with family, get a better job, go back to school, have an extended holiday, spend less money on work clothes, etc. Can you think of any more?

B) Someone cuts you off on the way home.

C) A tornado hits your community.

Change your Perception in 4 Steps

1. Change your energy

A) Get outside

If you are cooped up in the house, in bed or a hospital, try to get back to nature. Sit outside, go for a walk, open a window, bring in some plants, buy a tabletop waterfall, or listen to some nature sounds. I want you to do whatever you can do to bring nature into your life. Nature is healing and regenerative.

B) Change it up

We tend to be creatures of habit, and these habits can make our world small and our perceptions narrow.

If you spend your day in bed, change beds. If you spend your day in a chair, switch seats. If you spend your day in your house, go out somewhere. If you want to entertain new perceptions, you need to break out of your box or habitual ways of doing things.

C) Surround yourself with what you love

If your environment is cluttered with stuff, things that are not meaningful or pleasing to you, move them out or get rid of them. Replace them instead with what you love; photos, art, plants or natural objects. Make your environment supportive of positive energy and new positive perceptions.

D) Find your favorites

In this moment, identify your favorite, like your favorite chair, bed, breath, blanket, clothes, food, drink, etc. Choose the favorite in THIS MOMENT. Most likely it is the favorite in the moment. For example, my favorite chair is the one I am sitting in right now. How do I know? Because that's the only one I can sit in, in this moment. My favorite shirt? The one I am wearing. My favorite air? The air I am breathing. After finding your favorite after 5-10 minutes, you should notice a substantial shift in your energy. I got this idea from a YouTube video by

Abraham Hicks (2012), and it astonished me how easy it was to change my demeanor.

E) Music

Find soothing, gentle, positive music to play. Having a television on all day long or loud music playing does not support hearing your inner guidance. You have within you the answers you seek and new perceptions of your experience. It is important to create an environment conducive to hearing them.

F) Meditation

Meditation can be a powerful tool to train your mind and body to hear your inner guidance and see new perceptions and it does not require you to twist your legs into a pretzel and to have your fingers joined at the tips while sitting in an ashram in India. Meditation is simply the act of quieting the mind and allowing thoughts to pass through without investing in the stories attached to them. It can be done at home lying in bed, sitting in a chair or even while you walk through the woods. There are hundreds of resources including books, local groups, YouTube videos, meditation APP such as Headspace (www.headspace.com) or MP3 recordings to help you develop a meditation practice.

The first meditation I practiced was a breath meditation. I Imagined that I was breathing gently in and out through different parts of my body, gradually breathing into all of me.

First breathing into my toes and out through my toes, then......

Breathing into my toes, my ankles

....and out through my ankles and toes

Breathing into my toes, my ankles, my calves

....and out through my calves, ankles, and toes

Breathing into my toes, my ankles, my calves, my thighs

....and out through my thighs, calves, ankles, and toes

Breathing into my toes, my ankles, my calves, my thighs, my hips

....and out through my hips, thighs, calves, ankles, and toes

Breathing into my toes, my ankles, my calves, my thighs, my hips, and my stomach

..... and out through my stomach my hips, thighs, calves, ankles and toes

Breathing into my toes, my ankles, my calves, my thighs, my hips, my stomach, and into my chest

....and out through my chest, stomach, hips, thighs, calves, ankles and toes

Breathing into my toes, my ankles, my calves, my thighs, my hips, my stomach, chest and my shoulders

..... and out through my shoulders, chest, stomach, hips, thighs, calves, ankles, and toes

Breathing into my toes, my ankles, my calves, my thighs, my hips, my stomach, my shoulders, and down both arms

....and breathe up through both arms, through my shoulders, down through my chest, stomach, hips, thighs, calves, ankles, toes

Breathing into my toes, my ankles, my calves, my thighs, my hips, my stomach, my chest, my shoulders, arms and my neck

..... and out through my neck, arms, shoulders, chest, stomach, hips, thighs, calves, ankles, toes

Breathing into my toes, my ankles, my calves, my thighs, my hips, my stomach, my chest, my shoulders, arms, my neck and into my head

....and out through my head, neck, shoulders, arms, chest, stomach, hips, thighs, calves and toes

2. Question your perception

A) Can you absolutely know that it's true (Katie, 2002)?

When you have a perception of your life that seems absolutely horrible, question it. Can you absolutely know, with absolute certainty that it is true? For example,

- "My life is over." Is it really? You're alive right now.

- "I can't do anything." Really? You're reading this. You're breathing. You're aging.

B) What other possibilities could be true or truer?

If I had the thought, "My life is over because I have MD," what other possibilities could be true or truer?

- This is showing me what I am capable of.
- It's slowing me down to see what is really important.
- It's teaching me gratitude, recognizing all the good in my life.
- It's preparing me for an opportunity.
- I'm growing, expanding.

C) How can I see this differently?

See yourself from another's point of view. What are you bringing to the table because you are having this experience and what positive experiences can result from it?

- Gratitude for health, money, family, friends.
- Not taking things for granted.
- Moving forward in the face of adversity.
- Developing new skills.

D) How can I move that Polarity of Perception needle to the left?

Look at the diagram and find one alternative perception of the same experience and see if you can move that needle to the left. When you find one, find another, trying to move that needle farther and farther to the left. Before you know it you'll have 5-10 other possible perspectives of the same situation.

You're training your mind to open up and anticipate that there are always more ways of looking at the same situation.

3. Practice gratitude

A) What are you thankful for?

Invest in a journal and write down 5 things that you are grateful for when you wake up in the morning and then write 5 more before you fall asleep at night. Write 5 things now in the space below.

B) Brainstorm all the gifts that are in the experience.

What positive experience or experiences are you having as a result of this challenge that you would not have had without it? It could be that you don't have to go to work, follow a schedule, get more holidays, don't have to scrub floors, take the garbage out. Dig deep. They are there.

4. Break down the barriers

A. The illusion of safety

It can be frightening to consider other alternatives. The reason we feel so strongly about sticking with a particular perspective is because we have accumulated a vast array of evidence of how that perspective is true.

The problem arises, however, when those examples of proof accumulate without our knowledge. Like the case with my mother. On an unconscious level, I believed that it was safer not to move forward and seek alternatives to avoid the risk of having to ask for help and people leaving me. What that belief did, however, was keep me scared, limited and fearful of life.

B. Walk through fear

Fear has a way of limiting our choices. When we have one fear, we find other fears, and when we have other fears, we find more fears. Eventually, what happens is that our life becomes smaller and smaller, and our possibilities become fewer. You may start to develop a very narrow perspective of what your life is and what it can be especially when dealing with a disability or illness. Sometimes opening up to new possibilities or perspectives requires you to walk through a fear. That fear may be to try something new, do something a different way than you used to, or maybe accept help. No one can do this for you. As the Nike advertisement says, "just do it."

I could barely rise from a sitting position, used a walker and was constantly thinking about my next move. *Will I be able to get up? Is it slippery? Is it too crowded? Will they bump me? Concentrate. Don't get distracted. Don't fall.* This mind chatter went on all day. I was fearful of my next step.

I wanted to attend a conference in California. I knew it would be the best thing I could do for myself, but it scared the shit out of me. As I was sitting at the computer making the final payment for my registration my hands were shaking, my heart was exploding, and my mind was riddled with the reasons why I shouldn't do it. I contemplated whether or not I was going to throw up as I made the final click confirming my attendance.

I didn't know how I was going to manage to get, to and from the airport, carry my luggage or get around when I got there but I just did it anyway. I walked through the fear. I just did it. Terrifying? Yes. Overwhelming? Yes. But, as in most cases, the fear was all in my head, and everything turned out fine. In fact, that trip was the most significant and most transformative experience on my journey to freedom and connection within.

At some point, I had an inner urge to connect with a group of people who were exploring metaphysical topics, but our community seemed to be void of them. I noticed that two people brought up the idea of meetup.com. After the third time I heard about it, I knew it was something that I needed to do. That's how I heard my inner guidance. I noticed the messages because I was more present and aware.

I still remember sitting at the kitchen table filling in the information about the new group I was going to create called, "Manifesting the Connection." I planned the first event. A dinner at a restaurant and I would be the speaker. *What am I doing? Who am I to host something like this? No one will join. What if this is a big waste of money? I can't speak about this; I'm still learning. I must be crazy. What the hell am I doing?* But, I just did it anyway. I walked through the self-doubt and the fear, and committed with the click of the mouse.

Walking through fear requires a baby step forward. I didn't need to know all the details about the first event, the group dynamics, how I would fund it. I needed only to follow through with a single action moving me towards my goal: an, *in the moment* action. When that action was completed, I followed through with another one. At a certain point, your momentum carries you to the other side of fear, and that is where your hindsight reveals the truth. The thoughts that paralyzed you were just that. Thoughts.

Living your best life

You get one life. How you choose to experience the adventure is completely up to you. You are an incredibly powerful being having a unique experience. Do you want a life where you are overwhelmed by the problems, challenges, and stresses? Or, do you want a rockin', sit at the edge of your seat, didn't know it could be this awesome kind of life? It indeed is a choice. A matter of perspective.

CHAPTER EIGHT: FRIENDS AND LOVED ONES

HOW CAN FRIENDS AND LOVED ONES HELP SOMEONE WHO IS DEALING WITH A CHALLENGE?

1. Listen.

Really listen. Active listening requires you to concentrate on what the person going through the challenge is saying, without going into your thoughts searching for a response. Instead, concentrate only on what they are verbalizing to the point where you can feed it back to them as accurately as possible in summarized form. Once you feed back what they have shared with you, ask if that is what they said to confirm understanding. If they say yes, great.

If you want to help, ask, "Can I help you with that?"

If they ask you to help them, and it feels right for you, a feeling of love wanting to love without conditions, then do it. If it doesn't feel right, then don't.

2. Hold the space.

Showing up as a loving being requires nothing but showing up as a loving being. Holding a loving space for your loved one under any circumstance is the most authentic way for you to support them. In that space, you allow them to go through their challenge, whatever it is, without judgment. This is their journey and only they can move through it. Eckhart Tolle (2015), describes this non-reactivity as a wider version of forgiveness by seeing people as they really are, instead of as a personality or individual thinking and behaving from patterned beliefs.

Understanding the principle that every stressful thought a person experiences represents **their** issue that needs to be worked on, keeps you both from reinforcing each other's unconscious negative reactions.

If you feel you can be loving and hold the space, great. If you feel as if you can't in the moment, that is O.K. too. No one else is responsible for how you feel. Your loved one's challenge, and what it is doing to you, has nothing to do with the person with the challenge. Those are your limiting beliefs and yours alone. The experience is giving you the opportunity to question the patterned thoughts that keep you from joy and happiness.

If while supporting your loved one you get triggered, have a negative reaction, feel anxiety, stress or fear about their challenge or about something they have said or done, notice it and write it down. If you are no longer able to hold the space for your loved one because your mind is stressed or anxious, tell them. "I just got triggered. I need to take a minute and deal with it so that I can authentically be here for you."

As a support person you can also benefit from working through the, "4 Steps to increase your positive thoughts and decrease your negative thoughts," from Chapter Three or use the Worksheets from The Work of Byron Katie that can be found at www.thework.com.

Later on, when you are no longer triggered, you might want to share your experience with your loved one.

3. Don't feel guilty that your life is good.

You can help your loved one best by being authentic while he or she moves through this challenge because you can hold that loving space for them. The minute you start feeling guilty about being happy is the minute your attention and focus shifts, and you no longer can actively listen. I have often contemplated how some lives seemed ravished with challenges and others appeared to be completely unscathed. I began to see that everyone has an integral part to play in the Universe because we are all connected. As I heal, I heal the whole. Those people who appear to have the easy life become the safe place to fall for the others. We need them to be mentally, emotionally and physically available to support us. As they support us, they too, support the whole.

My sister was instrumental in my healing because she lovingly listened and helped me as I moved forward. When I called her crying, angry or scared, she gave me the opportunity to express my feelings, without judgment or advice giving me an avenue to release what I had so often buried inside. She encouraged me through her actions to ask for her help, to believe I was loved, cared for, valuable and helped me to reconnect with that loving presence that joined us both. She was part of the Universal support system that was always available and actively engaged but at times hidden from my view.

4. If you, the caregiver or loved one gets triggered it gives us the opportunity to hold the space for you.

Giving your loved one that option allows them to reconnect with who they really are. Loving you is loving themselves too. This is an opportunity for everyone to reconnect to who they really are because that is ultimately what all experiences are destined to do.

5. Be honest.

The loved one being supported might not like everything you say or do, but if **the loved one has a negative reaction**, that is **their** stuff to deal with. The same goes for you. If as the support person you don't like what your loved one says or does, and **you have an adverse reaction**, that's **your** stuff. If you are both courageous enough to take responsibility for your own thoughts and feelings, you can love one another, just as you are. You can experience the freedom of being less than perfect with the knowing that you are both doing the best you can with what you know at the time.

Ultimately, your journey together is about patching the cracks in your foundation of perception that keep you from, that which you really are, pure love. There is no faster way to identifying your limiting beliefs than immersing yourself in a stressful experience with the people you love because they tend to be your best triggers.

When my partner said, "I want a divorce. I can't handle you being disabled," I told everyone who would listen how terrible he was because he left me for no other reason than my ill health. What kind of human being leaves their spouse because he or she is sick? What I can see now is that he spoke his truth. He was honest. What I didn't realize at the time was that my tornado response indicated that I was triggered. I was projecting on to him what deep down I believed to be true. That if I could, I would do the same thing. I would divorce the illness because I couldn't deal with it either.

We never talked about what effect my illness had on his dreams, on his role in the family and how it triggered his limiting beliefs. He never opened up, giving me the opportunity to hold a loving space for him. I never felt comfortable bringing up the subject of illness because my pattern was not to ask for help, keep my feelings bottled up and put on the mask that everything was OK; I could handle it. That pattern started to develop when John teased me till I cried and no one helped me over and over again. The pattern grew in strength when I learned people couldn't handle my emotions, such as when Mom fell apart after my Dad died, and the minister came over and didn't identify or address my suicidal thoughts.

That and other unconscious patterns were running in the background of my relationship with my partner, and he had unconscious patterns that he brought to our marriage as well. Once we added the MD to the mix, the unconscious patterns got triggered trying to regain familiarity and balance.

Perhaps if we had been honest and shared our struggles with each other early on, we could have explored ways to move through the illness, finding the gifts in the experience together. We could have honored the loving beings that we both were by urging one another to speak their truth.

It seems ridiculous to me now that I wanted him to stay with me, even though he didn't want to. How would that conversation have gone? "I know you can't handle me being disabled, and you are in love with someone else, but you should stay with me. You should stay because my life would be easier if you did and nothing would have to change. I am going to tell you who you should love, and that person is me."

When you find fault or lack in someone else, that is an indication that you are no longer connected to source, and you have some work to do on yourself. Cleaning up limiting thought and belief patterns are the most loving things you can do for yourself and the most loving thing you do for those around you.

PRACTICE AND REFLECTION

1. When expressing yourself to others, try to notice any negative reactions you may be having. Do you feel angry? Does your body react? Do you shut down? Etc.

2. When you notice a negative reaction from those around you, observe, rather than engage. Notice the emotions and thoughts that arise within you as you observe their response. Defense, justification, blame, anger?

3. Make note of what triggers you. A word, a comment, the tone of their voice? What does that word, comment or tone of voice mean to you? What is the dialogue in your head that is attached to that word or comment? What does it say about you?

4. Actively listen to a friend or family member by concentrating on what they are saying so that you can paraphrase it back to them. Ask them questions for clarification and refrain from sharing a similar experience you may have had. Let the conversation be all about them.

    What was it like to actively listen? Did you feel differently physically? Emotionally? Mentally? What was their reaction to being deeply listened to? Record your experience.

∽✿∾

CHAPTER NINE:
CLARITY BRINGS CHOICE

It is perplexing to live life philosophically one way but respond in another, and I longed to figure out what it was that was keeping me from a life of peace and joy. The key to opening up infinite possibilities in my life was dependent on my ability to clear out the default patterns that were unconsciously collapsing possibility waves into a repetitive, predictable reality.

If we are operating 95% of the time from the unconscious mind, then the unconscious mind is automatically collapsing the wave of possibilities into a repetitive experience. When people suggest you are creating your experience, they are right. Based on quantum physics, the unconscious mind is creating your experience based on outdated, limited beliefs the nanosecond it has a thought because it only takes a thought to collapse the wave of possibilities. To increase your access to infinite possibilities you must clean up their subconscious (unconscious mind) and at the same time bring awareness to the present moment.

The law of attraction states that you need to put out into the universe that which you want, and imagine your life as though it has already happened. Seems easy enough. Why do so many people have difficulty manifesting what they want? Before they can even think the thought of what they want, they think about what they don't want. In other words, their unconscious mind puts out a thought immediately, of what they didn't want, and that thought (infused with emotion), automatically collapses the wave of possibilities. This all happens before the person has the thought of what they really want. Their free will (unconscious mind) was creating their experience from the confines of past experience. Infinite possibilities were there, but their free will was making them inaccessible, they were hidden. Therefore, to use the Law of Attraction effectively, you must love what you have first, then you can manifest something else.

Access to infinite possibilities requires a clear connection. This connection is obtained by cleaning up the outdated programs and reconnecting with who you really are. Who are you? Pure love. Pure source energy.

When you can live from a state of pure love, you love everything in your experience because you see it as yourself. That is happiness. Pure love observing pure love. To maximize your body's ability to heal and access infinite possibilities, you must make that reconnection. How do you do that? When you consciously choose to see the gifts in a situation, you are also choosing love. Even though your unconscious mind might be collapsing that wave automatically while you are practicing to see the gifts, you are doing what is required to create a new "go to," thought for the unconscious mind or creating a new habit. This new habit replaces the outdated limiting beliefs in the unconscious mind and thus, can begin to collapse the wave of possibilities in a new way.

The new loving habit is more open by its loving nature and can entertain more possibilities than its predecessor. The possibilities were always there, but now they are accessible to you. When one is living in a loving state, loving themselves, their experience and seeing the gifts moment to moment, I believe their will becomes in alignment with God's will. They see that God's loving plan has been and always will be, running in the background. We have always had the opportunity to see our lives as loving; it was only our thoughts that stopped us from doing so. When we clean up our foundation of perception, everyone appears as the loving being they are. Seeing my Mom as loving had nothing to do with my mother, and everything to do with me. Happiness is not dependent on anything outside of yourself. It really is an inside job.

If the essence of all that is (God, Universe, Source energy, peanut butter or whatever you want to call it), is everything, then everything is God. If God is perfect, then everything is perfect. If everything is perfect, then sickness is perfect, and only judgment makes it otherwise.

I invite you today, to look for the gifts in your life. They are there. With practice, you can make seeing the gifts your default, rather than allowing the unconscious, fear based perspectives that have been programmed by the past respond automatically. Lovingly embracing what is, would be more loving to your body, maximizing its potential to heal.

The journey is the journey, whether it is a journey to healing or a journey not to be healed the destination is the same. How do you want to experience it?

A LETTER HOME

When we realize the impact that our past (limiting beliefs) can have on our perception of today's experience, we can begin to entertain different perceptions and be open to more possibilities.

"Hi Mom, got a minute?" I asked.

"All the time in the world."

"I want to talk to you about something. I always feel like I need someone, like you needed Dad. To be there to take care of me to share things with so I am not alone. Like when.... Dad died or when you died, living alone above the flower store and being diagnosed with muscular dystrophy or the divorce ...the list goes on and on."

"You really have been through a lot without someone there to take care of you."

"I know that. I realize intellectually that I have done an amazing job of bouncing back and growing from my experiences, but it doesn't matter. Even though I do whatever I need to do to take care of things, to deal with it, deep down I still need someone."

"Is that true?"

"It feels like it's true because when I am alone and challenged, I crumble. But the crazy thing is I have shown over and over again I can totally meet each challenge head on and deal with it, yet my emotional, physical and mental response each time is always the same. I feel weak and beaten down having this insatiable need to have someone to take care of me or the situation and there's no one there who can do it."

"When I looked to your Father for my happiness, I believed it was him that I needed to take care of me, to feel happy, safe and secure, that's all I knew."

Instantly, I flashed to my mother, sitting in her red paisley chair, devastated, depressed and alone because my father, who always took care of her, was gone. She was incapable of believing she could do anything without him, and that is where I learned it too. I internalized that my happiness was dependent on someone taking care of me. Hundreds of examples seemed to flood in when I crumbled at the thought of working through something challenging on my own.

"And that's all I know."

"Yes, it appears so, until you know otherwise."

"What else is there to know Mom?"

"In death, it is so simple. I learned all that I wanted or needed was always there. What I wanted or needed was what I had. It can't be otherwise. It was my thinking that made me believe differently."

"So what you're saying is that I am always taken care of?"

"It appears so."

"And it is only my thinking, that I am not being taken care of, that makes me crumble?"

"It appears so,"

"That means that every time I crumbled I had an equal opportunity to feel taken care of, loved and happy. Each time I chose how to perceive the moment and each time I chose by default, to feel 'not taken care of,' regardless of my efforts to deal with it."

"Apparently."

"And I did this because this is how I learned to be in the world. This belief kept operating regardless of my efforts to think positively or to handle life's challenges as they came."

I let my words land, absorbing their meaning. That's exactly what happened every time. Before I took on a challenge, an overwhelming sense of devastation preceded it. These distressing times were exhausting, leaving me feeling depleted and haggard, incapable of going on. I always knew in my mind that I would get through it and that the answers would come, but my emotional response was always over the top and didn't match the circumstances.

"OMG! You know what that means? It means that I have a choice, right now and forever, to sit back and enjoy life, KNOWING, I am totally taken care of, always, no matter what happens."

"Yes, Lori, it's that simple."

"Do you realize how incredible that is? This enormous weight I've been carrying for my whole life feels like it has just lifted, I can breathe. Ahhh. It feels amazing."

She waited and allowed the new inner wisdom to take root. "Anything else you need before I go?" she asked.

Smiling, I took a long, deep, healing breath and lowered my pen. "No thanks. Everything is taken care of."

PRACTICE AND REFLECTION
The Happiness Toolbox

The Happiness Toolbox is your life. You have everything you need right now to find happiness regardless of what you are going through. Choose today to use the tools available to you, your life, your experiences, your reactions and non-reactions to draw you back to who you really are.

If the Universe or God could have a conversation with you it might go something like this.

UNIVERSE: I hear you are unhappy.
Use this experience as your tool to find happiness.
YOU: I don't want that.

UNIVERSE: OK. How about this experience?
YOU: I don't want that either.

UNIVERSE: How about this experience?
YOU: I need something different.

UNIVERSE: Like what?
YOU: I need more money.

UNIVERSE: I hear that you think the experience of having more money will make you happy but trust me, that is not what you need.
YOU: You don't know what you are talking about. I know more money will make everything easier.

UNIVERSE: I've got an amazing plan. A divine plan. A plan bigger and better than any plan you could ever imagine for yourself.
I've organized everything for you. Trust me.

YOU: I want my plan instead. I've got Free Will damn it and I have the right to use it.

UNIVERSE: That you do. I love you and want what you want.
YOU: I want to be happy.

UNIVERSE: I hear you are unhappy.
Use this experience as your tool to feel happy.
YOU: I don't want that.

UNIVERSE: OK. How about this experience?
YOU: I don't want that either.

UNIVERSE: How about this experience?
YOU: I need something different.

UNIVERSE: I've got an amazing plan. A divine plan. A plan bigger and better than any plan you could ever imagine for yourself. I've organized everything for you. Trust me.
YOU:

THE HAPPINESS PLAN

If you want to be happy regardless of circumstances, you need to take action. Below is a simple plan that you can use to begin to map out the actions you are willing to take to eliminate negative limiting beliefs, move through perceived barriers and enjoy life's journey without relying on external stimuli.

INDIVIDUAL HAPPINESS PLAN (EXAMPLE)

In the next week I want to work on: Not reacting negatively when I get triggered

What I want to accomplish this week is: Become aware of what is triggering me

I will use the following tools:

Positive affirmations		Find the gifts		Giving or doing something for someone else	
Thought alert (ex. dot on hand)		Ask, what are the facts?	✓	Emotional Vision Board	
Read		Bring awareness to my negative reactions	✓	Take action to elicit emotions	
Meditate		Identify connected thoughts	✓	Take responsibility for how I feel	✓
Question thoughts	✓	Inviting in what I resist or see as neg. in others	✓	Move the polarity perspective needle	
Change negative thoughts to positive thoughts		Mantra	✓	Go outside	
Empower positive thoughts		Awareness of Roles		Change my surroundings	

Gratitude journal		Letter from wiser future self		Find my favorites	
Hold the space for someone		Actively listen		Observe physical reaction	✓

The actions I will take are:

1. When I feel myself reacting, getting angry, I will not speak. I will bring my awareness to what I think I want to say, and write those thoughts down in the chart from chapter three. I will write down any physical sensations I feel as well.

2. I will use the chart to change the negative thoughts to positive thoughts and infuse them with emotion.

3. I will question my thoughts. Is it true? What are the facts? Is this something I am resisting in myself?

I know I will have made progress if: I do not react in anger in a stressful experience but instead reflect on what I am thinking, question my thinking and change those thoughts to positive thoughts.

The reason this plan is important to me is: I want to feel happy regardless of what happens outside of me.

INDIVIDUAL HAPPINESS PLAN TEMPLATE

1. In the next week I want to work on:

2. What I want to accomplish this week is:

3. I will use the following tools:

Positive affirmations		Find the gifts		Giving or doing something for someone else	
Thought alert (ex. dot on hand)		Ask, what are the facts?		Emotional Vision Board	
Read		Bring awareness to negative reactions		Take action to elicit emotions	
Meditate		Identify connected thoughts		Take responsibility for how I feel	
Question thoughts		Inviting in what I resist or see as negative in others		Move the polarity perspective needle	
Change negative thoughts to positive thoughts		Mantra		Go outside	
Empower positive thoughts		Awareness of Roles		Change my surroundings	
Gratitude journal		Letter from wiser future self		Find my favorites	
Hold the space for someone		Actively listen		Observe physical reactions	

The actions I will take are:

1)

2)

3)

I know I will have made progress if:

The reason this plan is important to me is:

QUESTIONS FROM READERS AND ANSWERS FROM AUTHOR

Question: Now that you have learned all this, are you happy all the time?

Most of the time I feel good. Sometimes I don't. When I don't feel good, I know I am believing something that is not true, and I question it. It usually has to do with me wanting reality to be different than what it is.

For instance, I caught myself wishing I could go on a boat with my family.

As soon as I felt my mood change, I asked, "What am I believing to be true?"

I was believing that I should be able to walk onto the boat. At that moment, I was not able to walk onto the boat, so I wanted reality to be different than what it was.

My mantra engaged, "If I am supposed to be going on the boat, I'd be able to get on it. If it is in God's Divine plan for me to take a boat ride, then I will be able to get on it. Until then, my reality in this moment is that I am not supposed to. I know that because I can't walk onto the boat.

Question: Do you consider yourself enlightened?

Sometimes I am enlightened and sometimes I am not. When I feel good and loving the present moment, I feel connected and in alignment with the Universe. When I feel bad, and I am wanting something to be different than what is, I am out of alignment and not enlightened. I don't believe enlightenment has a final destination. I believe enlightenment is an, "in the moment," experiential state of being. I am enlightened in the moment, or I am not.

Question: Do you consider happiness to be a choice?

Absolutely. Think of limiting thoughts as ice cream, if you're milk intolerant. Before you were told you had a dairy intolerance, you went about your life feeling good, feeling bad and feeling neutral believing it had to do with external circumstances.

One day you're told that you have a milk intolerance (limiting thoughts). If you ingest dairy, you won't feel good, and if you choose an alternative, you will feel good. You may still indulge in ice-cream even though you won't feel good afterward. It is a choice.

You might also choose to be unhappy by not taking action to do things differently and continuing to think the way you have always thought. It also is a choice.

Question: It appears that it took you a long time to get where you are. Does that mean it is going to take me that long?

I believe enlightenment (happiness) can happen every moment. If you project out into the future an idea of what needs to happen for you to be happy, then that in and of itself draws you away from happiness because you see happiness as out there, outside of yourself. If you are thinking, "I want to be like you." In this moment, you can be. You can be connected and aligned or not connected. You and I have the same choice in every moment.

If you are connected, and aligned you feel good.

If you are not connected and aligned, it doesn't feel good.

You choose to be connected.

Question: Easy for you to say. What if something really bad happens, how do you get connected?

Go back to, "Change your perception in 4 steps," and do as many steps as it takes to change how you feel. Your feelings are a beacon to connection.

Question: I have read the book, but I still have a hard time finding the gifts when I am feeling crappy. Why is that?

One moment at a time, find one gift. Find your favorite. Remember, you are wired to keep things the same. Change requires some action to move you forward. Reading the book is not enough. Engaging in the exercises and implementing the strategies into your life on a daily basis is necessary to create a new habit.

Question: Why did I get sick? Why me?

Illness, pain, limitation is the same as a bad relationship, money issues, frustration, aging, and whatever else results in a negative response. They are all tools. They are not good, or bad they are just tools that the Universe uses to bring you back home. You are having an experience. How you respond to the experience is entirely up to you. Unconscious or conscious. Loving it or hating it, neutral or in awe of it. There is no right or wrong way to respond, but if you are going to have the experience, would it not be more fun to love it?

Question: Do you forgive your mother?

There is nothing to forgive. When we clean up our filter, patch our foundation of perception or remove the veil, everyone appears as the loving being they are. Seeing my Mom as loving had nothing to do with my mother, and everything to do with me.

Question: I don't feel good but can't figure out what is making me feel this way.

What is your mind saying to keep you from going back to, Change your perception in 4 steps? Your mind is trained to keep you from taking that action. Just thinking about how you want things to change is not going to create any movement forward. Change requires action.

ᴄ◯◯ᴄ

BOOK CLUB COMPANION

Introduction – Chapter Two

1. Have you tried to change your thinking? If so, what strategy did you use? Was it successful? If not, why do you think it was not successful?

2. Have you had an experience where other people wanted to fix you or tell you how to be happier?

   If so, what did they suggest? Did you try it? If so, did it work?

3. What Positive or Negative information have you absorbed from childhood? What beliefs do you have about money, roles of men or women, work, life, etc., that were taught to you growing up? (For example,

money doesn't grow on trees, children are to be seen not heard, you can accomplish anything you set your mind on, etc.)

4. In the introduction, Lori Brant states, "Loving yourself and everything in your experience entirely, dissolves the judgment of circumstances as good or bad. Once you love everything in your experience, the need for anything to change no longer exists." Do you think it's possible to love everything? Why or why not?

5. What does, "Pure love sees only pure love in its reflection," mean to you?

Chapter Three

1. "A belief is a thought with emotion(s) attached to it. Belief patterns form when we interpret what we experience and file it away in our memory like files in a filing cabinet. As we decode more and more experiences, our mind creates files by bunching similar experiences together finding generalities and commonalities amongst them. These files make up our subconscious or unconscious mind, a culmination of general ways to respond to similar situations or the foundation of

our perception." What general ways do you respond to challenging circumstances?

2. "Identifying the thoughts or beliefs that hold up or maintain your fear is a vital step for you to be able to challenge those thoughts, head on." What strategy did you use to identify what you were thinking? Was it helpful? If so, explain. If not, explain why.

3. During a negative reaction have you been able to get out of the details and uncover the facts? If so, did it change how you perceived the situation?

Did it change how you were feeling?

Did you have any difficulties sticking to the facts, and if so, what made it difficult?

4. From the practice and reflection section of Chapter Three,

Were you able to identify any negative thoughts? If not, why?

What negative thoughts did you catch yourself saying?

Were you able to turn a negative thought into a positive thought? If so, was it helpful? If not, why?

Were you able to positively charge the positive thought by finding examples of how it was true for you? What was your experience while doing that? What did it feel like? Was it easy? Difficult?

Did you make any connections between your negative thoughts?

5. With a partner or in your group, did you find any commonalities between your negative thoughts?

6. Unresolved feelings or negative beliefs from the past can be triggered by an experience you have today, creating an exaggerated reaction. Have you ever experienced an exaggerated response?

How could you use the tools and strategies discussed in Chapter Three to deal with an exaggerated response or a situation where you find yourself reacting negatively?

7. "Mirroring is a way in which the Universe shows us our belief patterns by reflecting back to us what needs to be worked on, identifiable by our reaction.

1. That which we hate in others is what we deny most within ourselves.

2. That which we deny within us, we believe to be true."

Any adverse reaction, stressful thought, annoyance, etc. is your neon sign or tool, telling you that a limiting belief is active within you. Unconsciously, a file gets triggered, firing off the programmed emotional response showing up in the moment as stress, annoyance, judgment, etc."

Did you identify any instances where someone was mirroring back to you what you need to work on within yourself? Explain.

What reaction did you have finding where that belief was true for you in Chapter 3, Exercise 3? "

(Chapter Three, Exercise Three)

Chapter Four

1. How does fear impact you emotionally, mentally, or physically?

2. Discuss as a group how you can use the information from chapters 1-4, to work through fear. Create a plan of action to deal with a fear.

3. What obstacles would prevent you from implementing the plan to deal with fear? How can you deal with those obstacles so you can work through fear?

4. Share your mantra with the group.

5. What was it like hearing everyone's mantra?

Chapter Five

1. Consider and share what emotional, mental or physical rewards or benefits you receive from your Job, Friendships, Family, Leisure/Community or Spiritual/religious connections?

2. Now that you have considered how your identity may be affected by roles and role changes how can you use that information moving forward?

3. Have you taken on a new role? Discuss.

4. Discuss societal, cultural and familial pressures to engage in roles and fulfill the expectations of roles.

5. Who are you? Can you answer that without using roles to identify yourself?

6. Share your reflections, thoughts or insights after reading your letter from your wiser self fifteen years in the future.

Chapter Six

1. How can you work towards a goal or dream without becoming attached?

2. "Have you heard the expression, "finding your passion?" The underlying belief is that everyone has something here on earth that they were destined to do, and when they find it, they'll be happy." Do you think it is possible to find passion in everything you do? Discuss.

3. Share your plan to experience your dream today with the group.

    a. Share your dream

    b. Share what thoughts and emotions you think you will feel when you reach your dream?

    c. Share what thoughts and emotions you think others will feel about you when you reach your dream?

    d. What did you identify as your top 5 emotional rewards for achieving your dream?

e. What actions could you take to elicit those feelings within you today?

f. Did you do it? If so, share. If not, share why.

Chapter Seven

1. Discuss, "Are you really *in control*? Or do you feel in control when your outside experiences are a match to what you want, and then feel *not in control*, when outside experiences don't match what you want?"

2. "If you practice finding the gifts in the moment, this can become your default response in all cases."

   As a group can you find the potential gifts in the following experiences;

   a. Losing a thousand dollars.

   b. Camping in the rain.

   c. Having a flood in your home.

3. If you are having difficulty seeing the gifts in an experience, have the group brainstorm with you to find potential gifts you may not be able to see.

4. Discuss, "It is possible to have the gift of hindsight by consciously choosing to see the gifts in every experience. Our freedom comes from opening up our perception of reality to the gifts in each moment and consciously making the effort to do so. We can do the same thing with past, negative memories too. You can't change what happened to you, but you can change your perception of it."

5. Practice the breathing meditation for Practice and Reflection # 1 (F). Play gentle music in the background or practice the meditation in silence as one member reads it slowly and soothingly.

   Discuss the meditation. How did it feel? Was it beneficial? Any difficulties?

Chapter Eight

1. In partners, have one person share their challenge or negative experience while the other person practices to actively listen. Set a timer for five minutes.

   a. What was it like to have someone actively listen to you?

   b. As the listener, what was the experience like for you?

c. What benefits do you see in actively listening to the people in your life?

2. Discuss, "Understanding the principle that every stressful thought a person experiences represents **their** issue that needs to be worked on, keeps you both from reinforcing each other's unconscious negative reactions."

3. Triggers. As a group create a general plan to deal with situations where you are triggered by what someone says or does resulting in a negative response within you. For example, the first step might be to count to 10 in your head.

Chapter Nine

1. "When one is living in a loving state, loving themselves, their experience and seeing the gifts moment to moment, I believe their will becomes in alignment with God's will." Discuss.

2. "If the essence of all that is (God, Universe, Source energy, peanut butter or whatever you want to call it), is everything, then everything is God. If God is perfect, then everything is perfect. If everything is perfect, then sickness, divorce, death is perfect, and only judgment makes it otherwise." Discuss.

3. In partners, help each other create a Happiness Plan for the upcoming week.

If it is your desire to be happy regardless of outside circumstances, go to **http://www.loribrant.com/** or email *contactloribrant@gmail.com to learn more about one on one coaching.*

If you are a health care practitioner or Life Coach, interested in learning how you can support your clients dealing with limiting beliefs, please go to http:// www.loribrant.com/ for more information.

BIBLIOGRAPHY

Braden, G. (2008). *Spontaneous healing of belief*: shattering
   the paradigm of false limits. New York, New York, USA: Hay
   House.

Chopra, D. (2004). *Fire in the Heart*. New York: Simon &
   Schuster Books for Young Readers.

Dyer, W. W. (2007). *Change your thoughts, change your life.*
   Carlsbad, CA: Hay House Publishing.

Dyer, W. (2004). *The power of intention*. Carlsbad, California,
   USA: Hay House Inc.

Dyer, W. (1993). *Real magic*. New York, New York,
   USA: HarperCollinsPublishers.

Expectation. (n.d.) In Wikipedia. Retrieved February 11, 2016,
   from https://en.wikipedia.org/wiki/ Expectation_(epistemic)

Feinberg, C. (2013). *The placebo phenomenon*. Retrieved from
   http://harvardmagazine.com/ 2013/01/the-placebo-phenomenon.

Flight or Fight Response. (n.d.) In Wikipedia. Retrieved February 21, 2016
   from https://en.wikipedia.org/wiki/Fight-or-flight_response

Hay, L. (1988). *You can heal your life*. Carlsbad, California, USA: Hay
   House Inc.

Hendricks, G and K. (1990). *Conscious loving: The journey to
   co-commitment*. New York: Bantam Books.

Hicks, E. (2012) *Abraham Hicks – Name your ten favorite things.*
   Retrieved from https://www.youtube.com/watch?v=1bSouFyDn_Y

Hicks, E. and J. Hicks. (2008). *Money and the law of attraction.* New York, New York, USA: Hay House.

Hicks, E. and J. Hicks. (2006). *The amazing power of deliberate intent.* New York: Hay House.

Kaptchuk, T. J., Stason, W. B., Davis, R. B., Legedza, A. T. R., Schnyer, R. N., Kerr, C. E., ... Goldman, R. H. (2006). *Sham device versus inert pill: Randomized controlled trial of two placebo treatments. BMJ: British Medical Journal, 332*(7538), 391–394. Retrieved from http://www.jstor.org.libproxy.wlu. ca/stable/25456159

Katie, B. (2009). *The School for The Work.* Performer, October. Crowne Plaza, Los Angeles, California, USA.

Katie, B. (2009). *Loving What Is.*(Performer, October 2-4), Toronto Convention Center, Toronto, Ontario, Canada.

Katie, B. (2007). *Catching up with reality: An interview with Byron Katie.* Ojai, California, USA.

Katie, B. (2007). *Question your thinking, change the world.* Carlsbad, CA: Hay House Publishing.

Katie, B. (2002). *Loving what is.* New York, New York, USA: Three Rivers Press.

Lally, P., Van Jaarsveld C.H.M., Potts, H.W.W., Wardle, J. (2010). How are habits formed: modelling habit formation in the real world. European Journal of Social Psychology. 40, 998-1009.

Langley, S. (2012). *The neuroscience of change: Why it's difficult and what makes it easier.* Neuroconnections, March 23. Available at: http://blog.langleygroup.com.au/ neuroscience-of-change-what-makes-change-easier/

Lipton, B. (2005). *The biology of belief.* Santa Rosa, California, USA: Mountain of Love/Elite Books.

Lipton, B. (2007). *http://www.brucelipton.com/article/mind-growth-matter.* (J. Fraser, Ed.) Retrieved 06 01, 2009, from http://www.brucelipton.com: http://www.brucelipton.com/ article/mind-growth-matter

Lipton, B. (2008). *The intelligence of cells.*]Paper. Originally published in Peak Vitality: (2008). Raising the threshold of abundance in our material, spiritual and emotional lives. Editor: J. M. House, Elite Books, Santa Rosa, CA.

Lipton, B. (2008). Interview with Wayne Dyer and Bruce Lipton Phd. December 11. (W. Dyer, Interviewer) PBS.

Lipton, B. (2008, October 9) *Talk for food . Adam welcomes Dr. Bruce Lipton on 'The new biology'*. (A. Abraham, Interviewer)

Mayo Clinic Staff. (2013). *Stress symptoms: Effects on your body and behavior*. Retrieved from http://www.mayoclinic.org/healthy-lifestyle/stress-management/in-depth/stress-symptoms/art-20050987?pg=1

McGraw, P. (2000). *Relationship rescue*. New York, New York, USA: Hyperion Press.

Myss, C. (1996). *Anatomy of the spirit*. New York, New York, USA: Three Rivers Press.

Sandlin, D. (2015). *The backwards brain bicycle*. Retrieved from Smarter Everyday https://www.youtube.com/watch?v=MFzDaBzBlLo

Schwabe, L., Wolf, OT. (2013). Stress and multiple memory systems: from "thinking" to "doing" Trends Cognitive Science. 17:60-68.

Tolle, E. (2005). *A new earth. Awakening to your life's purpose*. New York, NY: Penguin Group.

Tolle, E. (2015). *The meaning of forgiveness. Taken from Where do the wonderful things in my life come from. Retrieved from* http://acimlounge.ning.com/video/where-do-the-wonderful-things-in-my-life-come-from-eckhart-tolle

Walker, I, Thomas GO, Verplanken B. (2014). Old habits die hard:travel habit formation and decay during an office relocation. Environmental. Behavior. doi: 10.1177/0013915614549619

APPENDIX

Abraham-Hicks © by Jerry & Esther Hicks, contact:http://www.abraham-hicks.com; (830) 755-2299.

Bruce H. Lipton, Ph.D. contact: www.brucelipton.com.

Feinberg, C. (2013). Cara Feinberg is a journalist working in print and documentary television. She can be reached at http://www.CaraFeinberg.com.

Gregg Braden contact: Wisdom Traditions, Office of Gregg Braden, PO Box 14668, North Palm Beach, Florida 33408, 561.799.9337, Email: info@greggbraden.com, Web: www.greggbraden.com.

Oprah Winfrey contact http://www.oprah.com

CPSIA information can be obtained
at www.ICGtesting.com
Printed in the USA
LVOW01s2348190516
489127LV00013B/80/P